Breakfast at Tiffany's

The Official Guide to Style

Breakfast at Tiffany's

The Official Guide to Style

OVER 100 FASHION, DECORATING, AND ENTERTAINING TIPS
TO BRING OUT YOUR INNER HOLLY GOLIGHTLY

WRITTEN BY *Caroline Jones*   ILLUSTRATED BY *Sophie Griotto*

INSIGHT
EDITIONS

San Rafael • Los Angeles • London

Contents

Introduction

For six decades, millions have watched *Breakfast at Tiffany's* and ached to be as effortlessly stylish as Holly Golightly. From the iconic black Givenchy dress, pearls, and oversize sunglasses she wears in the opening scene to the men's formal dress shirt and blue eye mask she slips on when she first meets Paul Varjak, every look Holly wears makes an indelible impression and continues to exert a huge influence on our fashion tastes today.

But this timeless appeal is about more than the undeniably fabulous clothes—it's the entire movie's style ethos that still captivates modern audiences. Every detail sparkles, from Holly's famous tiara-adorned party hairstyle to her oh-so-'60s smoky cat eye. And of course no celebration of the film's aesthetic would be complete without a well-deserved nod to the eccentric boho chic of her Manhattan brownstone apartment—the scene of Holly's memorably hip cocktail soiree.

Perhaps key to the character's lasting appeal is that Holly isn't just a clotheshorse—she is a fully realized character, a vivacious yet sensitive woman with a wide-eyed enthusiasm for life and spontaneity that is infectious. As Holly breezes through 1960s New York, she teaches us that women can have both self-respect and personal style—whatever their income—and that it's okay to break the rules sometimes. Through her unique blend of confidence and vulnerability, we learn the importance of embracing your inner Holly Golightly *and* Lula Mae Barnes, the innocent childhood alter ego Holly attempted to leave behind when she fled Texas to reinvent herself as a society girl in New York.

Style for Holly is a reflection of her inner strength—dressing up is a ritual that gives her mood a boost and allows her bubbly personality to shine through. When life gets tough, she slips on a fabulous gown to feel better—something many of us can relate to.

With so much inspiration on show, it's no wonder the character has proved such an enduring influence for generations. This easy-to-follow guide offers practical, budget-friendly advice for adding *Breakfast at Tiffany's* chic to all your wardrobe, home decor, and entertaining endeavors. While it's impossible to time-travel back to 1961, you can sprinkle that Golightly elegance into the style choices you make today.

How to Use This Book

This book is divided into five chapters, each containing the tips and tricks you need to incorporate a dash of Holly Golightly's timeless style into every aspect of your life. While Holly herself is a free spirit who thrives on spontaneity, channeling some of her essence into your busy life takes a touch more thought and preparation. But the good news is that we've made it easy with detailed instructions that will help you every step of the way.

Of course, living like Holly is more complex than just a style blueprint, so we've included some of her famous quotes and words of advice to further inspire you to adapt her carefree joie de vivre. Plus, there are plenty of ways to make each look your own.

At the end of each chapter, you'll find two pages with space for you to jot down notes, tips, and tricks for how you've made each look unique to your own personal style and tastes. Enjoy!

HOLLY'S FABULOUS FASHION

In the first chapter, we explain how to source Holly's capsule wardrobe, which will help you unlock the versatile style that is such a strong part of her character.

If you're looking to assemble an outfit, you'll find five easy-to-follow tutorials for creating your personal version of the movie's iconic ensembles. As you'll see, it's not about dressing up as Holly but about learning to emulate her effortless chic while adding your own modern twist.

And for finishing touches, the accessories guide shows you how to channel Holly's clever and creative use of shoes, jewelry, and handbags to transform your evergreen fashion staples.

BLUSH-WORTHY BEAUTY

Our beauty chapter takes you step-by-step through five simple but stylish makeup tutorials, each designed to help you create your version of Holly's key looks. Discover the secret to long-lasting party makeup that still looks fresh the next morning (in case the party goes all night!). Learn the subtle art of Holly's natural no-makeup makeup look. Shopping for retro beauty essentials? Walk through Holly's powder room and take a look at the skin-care products and nutrition tips that will help you achieve her gorgeous, glowing skin.

HOLLYWOOD HAIR

In Chapter 3, you'll find everything you need to rock four of Holly's heavenly hairstyles, with tips on how to bring each look up to the moment. In these easy step-by-step tutorials, you'll discover how to style a wearable baby beehive as well as how to achieve the ultimate Golightly evening updo all by yourself—no hairdresser required! You'll also find advice on hair products and even on foods to eat to help you maintain your crowning glory.

"I'LL TAKE MANHATTAN" DREAM DECOR

There's no place quite like Holly's New York apartment, and in this chapter, you'll learn how to introduce a dash of her quirky chic into your own home—without spending a fortune. Easy-to-follow DIY projects include how to upcycle an old bathtub into a statement sofa just like Holly's! If you're after something a bit simpler, our shopping guide shows you how best to add those little vintage touches, such as an old dial-up phone or a zebra-print rug.

GOLIGHTLY ENTERTAINING

Holly's talk-of-the-town gatherings may look thrown together on a whim, but the guarantee of a great party is attention to detail, which is why this chapter includes comprehensive guides on how to throw three *Breakfast at Tiffany's*–themed parties Holly would be proud of.

From the perfect cocktail evening to a sparkling champagne brunch, each of our party guides includes step-by-step suggestions for recipes, decor, gift bags, and more. All these ingredients and ideas are easy to source, but remember, like all the tips in this book, our party templates are just suggestions, so stick to them only as closely as suits you. If you want to add your own twist, go for it—Holly certainly would!

So, if you're ready to discover your inner Holly Golightly, let's start re-creating some of that *Breakfast at Tiffany's* movie magic!

Holly's Fabulous Fashion

It's hard to imagine a movie that's had a more lasting impact on fashion trends than *Breakfast at Tiffany's*. Many of Holly Golightly's looks, designed for the film by Hubert de Givenchy, continue to be celebrated as well as copied to this day, including her little black dress and oversize sunglasses, both firmly established in the modern style lexicon.

Bewitching yet beguilingly simple, Holly's outfits remain a shorthand for effortless chic, offering stylish lessons in versatility for every smart dresser today.

In this chapter, we focus on key wardrobe pieces and share how to create your own versions of the film's most memorable fashion moments.

"I am a very stylish girl!"

Holly's Capsule Wardrobe: Five Evergreen Fashion Staple Must-Haves

One of the clever style threads that runs throughout *Breakfast at Tiffany's* is the recycling of items in Holly's wardrobe. It makes perfect sense that a struggling city girl would work with a limited repertoire—back in 1961, fast fashion didn't exist, and only the very wealthy could wear something different every day. Aspiring young women owned far fewer items of clothing, so the pieces they chose were carefully selected, of good quality, and well taken care of. Holly deftly makes each reappearing piece look fresh every time, thanks to smart accessory changes, such as adding a feathered pillbox hat, a colored scarf, or some statement earrings. And with modern fashion's new focus on ethical sourcing and sustainability, a closet based on quality over quantity is a style philosophy that makes perfect sense today. Holly's approach echoes the classic European strategy of a capsule wardrobe—a small but perfectly curated collection of key pieces that can be mixed and matched to form a wide range of beautiful outfits.

Here, five starter items you need for a capsule wardrobe based on Holly Golightly's style.

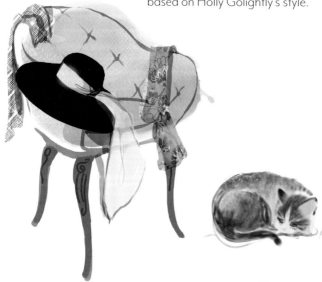

1 The Little Black Dress

Back in 1926, iconic fashion designer Coco Chanel debuted a simple black dress in *Vogue* and started the LBD craze. But it was Holly Golightly who showcased the versatility of the little black dress, instantly making it a wardrobe essential.

The eagle-eyed may spot that Holly actually has two black Givenchy dresses in the film, but one or the other is worn in almost every scene—from breakfast on Fifth Avenue to a trip to Sing Sing prison to cocktails at 21. And yet, with only a quick change of accessories, the dresses manage to look unique with each wearing.

The first, worn in the famous early-morning opening scene as Holly steps out of a yellow New York taxi and gazes into Tiffany & Co.'s shop window, is a straight-lined, black satin gown with a beautiful ornate cutout back. Holly wears it with long black satin gloves, pearls, and sunglasses. In a later cocktail party scene, the same dress is transformed when teamed with earrings and a simple long white silk scarf.

The second *petite robe noire* is in cloque silk with a slightly flared, frilly skirt, which Holly wears with a large wide-brimmed hat trimmed with a thick cream silk scarf, low-heeled alligator shoes, long gloves, and another pair of oversize sunglasses. Both dresses demonstrate the dawn-to-dusk adaptability that has been a huge part of the appeal of the LBD ever since Holly popularized it. Indeed, the very beauty of the perfect little black dress is that it can be endlessly adjusted to suit mood, season, or time of day.

GET THE LOOK

Simplicity is key. Look for long, clean lines, and choose a cut that fits you like a glove, whatever your size and shape—this isn't the time for loose and flowing. Sleeveless with wide straps or a boatneck guarantees a retro Holly vibe. Opt for a style that nips in at the waist to create shape and a sharp silhouette. The fabric should be sturdy cotton twill, silk, or heavy jersey—something that will hold its form.

2 Perfect Hat

When Holly first meets Paul Varjak, she wows him with her speedy transformation from sleepwear to stunningly stylish girl about town. "How do I look?" she asks. "Very good. I must say, I'm amazed," replies a shell-shocked Paul. The reason for Holly's quick change is she's late to visit Mafia boss Sally Tomato in Sing Sing prison—an occasion for which, she tells Paul, it's important to dress up: "All the visitors make an effort to look their best. Actually, it's very touching, all the women wearing their prettiest things."

Holly's prison outfit is a simple one consisting of black dress and shoes, but it's her enormous *chapeau du matin* (morning hat) that steals the show. The eye-catching wide saucer brim provides the perfect contrast to Holly's small, delicate features and tiny frame. Adding to the oversize effect is the incredibly long white silk scarf tied around the hat's base. The hat with scarf adds an air of mystery and glamour to her simple, formfitting dress. It's a dramatic look that's both bold and timeless and one that fashion designers have emulated ever since.

GET THE LOOK

A wide-brimmed showstopper of a hat can be your best friend—whether you are lounging on the beach, going to a wedding, or spending a day at the horse races, so it's worth putting some time and effort into finding a good one. Again, style doesn't mean having to spend a fortune. Secondhand hats are something thrift stores almost always have in stock. Choose a black base for versatility, and the bigger the better. Keep a variety of scarves, brooches, and ribbons on hand to vary the look and increase the impact. Wear it Holly-style, with confidence and your head held high.

3 Classic Trench Coat

The famous final scene in *Breakfast at Tiffany's*, when Holly finally admits her love for Paul, is a heart-stopping moment. With the rain pouring down, a drenched Holly looks stunning in a simple beige raincoat designed by Burberry, the celebrated British luxury fashion house founded in 1856. Indeed, many style experts credit this as the moment when trench coats were elevated from simple wet-weather protection to become a must-have for all style-conscious women. Even today, the perfect trench is a shorthand way to add understated chic to any outfit—a stylish staple for everyone from *Sex and the City*'s Carrie Bradshaw to British actresses Emma Watson and Cara Delevingne. Timeless and wearable, a trench works hard for your wardrobe 24/7, whether you're hanging in the park or dressing up for a smart lunch date.

GET THE LOOK

Holly's Burberry coat is still in production, but it remains an eye-wateringly expensive option at around $2,000. Thankfully, its now-classic shape has spawned countless copycats, with affordable brands issuing their own versions every year—making the trench another look that's easy to emulate without breaking the bank. It's also worth hunting through your local thrift store or checking out online auction sites for a good-quality secondhand coat—you might even strike gold and find a genuine vintage Burberry at a bargain price!

TOP TIP

Seeking a bargain? It's worth trawling through thrift stores for a good-quality piece—or even hunting through the wardrobes of your mom, your friends, or older relatives for vintage gems (with permission, of course!).

4 Oversize Sunglasses

In daylight hours, Holly is always seen sporting enormous sunglasses, usually the large tortoiseshell Oliver Goldsmith pair she wears in the movie's opening scene. For Holly, shades serve to hide a multitude of sins—including very late nights and occasionally a few tears, such as when she's jilted by her Brazilian fiancé, José da Silva Pereira. And as many a stylish celebrity has discovered, the right sunglasses have a magical way of conferring instant mystery and glamour to any outfit.

GET THE LOOK

Stylish sunglasses are another item you needn't spend a fortune on to look the part. Large designer shades may be tempting but can cost several hundred dollars, whereas you can pick up a decent off-the-shelf oversize pair in just about any store—often for less than ten dollars. And don't be shy—bigger is definitely better when it comes to frames. Cat-eyes are perfect for rocking retro '60s chic, ideally in classic black or tortoiseshell for maximum homage to Holly.

5 The Capri Pants

The final evergreen style staple Holly
helped popularize is the cropped pant. In
the film, she wears them dressed down
with a boatneck camel sweater and ballet
flats. Capri pants (also known as cigarette
pants for their straight cut) are a classic
1950s trouser with a high waist, a side or
back zipper, flat front, slanted pocket, wide
waistband, and slim-fitting legs that graze
the ankle. The name is derived from the
Italian island of Capri, where they rose to
popularity in the late 1950s.

When capris were first created, pants
on women were still quite a novelty, and
so capris were designed to be a chic, sleek
alternative to a skirt. Smart enough for the
office but casual enough for a trip downtown,
they confer instant sophistication and look
great paired with everything from sweaters
to smart blouses to striped Breton tops.

GET THE LOOK

An eternally popular style, capri pants
can be found at most price points. A key
element to remember when choosing the
perfect cropped pants is getting the right
fabric quality to create an elegant drape.
Heavy cotton twill or a very fine wool
works well and should have a crisp and
neatly pressed finish—you'll want to avoid
creases or a loose fit.

Five Golightly Looks to Love

Follow these easy guides to channel some Holly Golightly chic and put together your own versions of the most memorable outfits in *Breakfast at Tiffany's*.

 1 Holly's First Little Black Dress

THE OUTFIT

This scene may be set in early morning, but when Holly steps out of a yellow cab onto a deserted Fifth Avenue outside Tiffany & Co., she is sporting the ultimate evening look—the one everyone thinks of when recalling the movie.

The iconic black dress is by designer Hubert de Givenchy. It's a sleeveless, long gown with a neckline designed to accentuate Holly's slim, sculpted shoulders. The *demi-lune* (half-moon) cutout shape at the back adds a sexy edge, but it's the accessories that really bring it to life: over-the-elbow gloves, large tortoiseshell Oliver Goldsmith sunglasses, a Tiffany & Co. multistrand pearl necklace, and striking tiara-style crystal hair ornament.

WHERE TO WEAR

A black-tie ball, gala, or other special occasion

WHAT YOU'LL NEED

- Formfitting mid- or floor-length black evening dress that makes you feel fabulous
- Black kitten heels
- Multistrand imitation pearl necklace
- Crystal earrings
- Oversize dark-framed sunglasses
- Black over-the-elbow evening gloves
- Jeweled hair comb or slide
- White shawl or pashmina

EXTRAS

A white paper bag complete with a takeout pastry and coffee!

"You could always tell what kind of a person a man thinks you are by the earrings he gives you."

HOW TO STYLE IT

Avoid scouring fancy dress shops for a like-for-like copy of the dress—as long as it's black, formfitting, and you feel good in it, you'll be able pay homage to Holly without looking too similar. The same goes for the jewelry—something made of pearl or crystals is enough to create the right vibe; it doesn't have to be exactly the same. If, as for most of us, real pearls are out of the question, you can pick up some great imitations in department stores. And thrift stores really come into their own when you're looking for vintage faux pearls in bold '50s or '60s designs. Accessorize to make the outfit your own.

FUN FACT

Three copies of the original Givenchy dress worn by Holly in this famous scene were made for the movie. One of them sold at auction house Christie's in New York in 2006 for $923,187, making it one of the most expensive pieces of film memorabilia ever sold!

2 Holly's Dressed-Down Chic

THE OUTFIT
As Holly plays guitar and sings "Moon River" on the fire escape, she sports three-quarter-length blue jeans, black flats, a gray sweater, and a white turban-style cloth around her hair. This outfit was created by the movie's chief costume supervisor—the renowned Edith Head—and the relaxed look has proved just as timeless as her little black dress.

WHERE TO WEAR
Brunch with friends, a daytime picnic

WHAT YOU'LL NEED
- Slim-fitting, medium-wash cropped blue jeans
- Black ballet flats, ideally with a pointed toe
- Gray boyfriend-style sweatshirt
- Hair turban or '50s-style hair band

EXTRAS
Secondhand acoustic guitar. This is a great excuse to learn how to play if it's been on your bucket list.

HOW TO STYLE IT
The trick is to channel a retro vibe here, so the most important things are that the jeans are cropped above the ankle, the shoes flat, and that you have an appropriate hair accessory to finish off the classic look. Luckily, in recent times, '50s-inspired ready-styled head wraps have become a fashionable accessory and can be purchased inexpensively in many stores. Otherwise any pretty silk scarf tied around the hair and knotted on top of the head will work.

FUN FACT
The song "Moon River" was written by American composer Henry Mancini just for the movie. A wistful, nostalgic song, it shows party girl Holly's private side and hints at her true Southern roots, growing up in Texas as Lula Mae Barnes.

"It may be normal, darling; but I'd rather be natural."

3 The Pretty-in-Pink Party Dress

THE OUTFIT
Upon returning from dinner with fiancé José, Holly is dressed in a show-stopping Givenchy-designed hot pink silk cocktail dress studded with green rhinestones and with a pink bow around the waist. The gown is teamed with a collarless three-quarter-sleeved coat in the same vibrant hue.

WHERE TO WEAR
Cocktail party or prom

WHAT YOU'LL NEED
· Slim-fit pink dress with a belted waist; the skirt can be full but not too wide
· Cropped jacket or fine-knit cardigan in a matching shade of pink
· Pink satin kitten heels or similar
· Pink crystal earrings and a similar hair comb or repurposed necklace—the bigger the better!

EXTRAS
White or pink rectangular evening clutch, ideally beaded or sequined like the one Holly carries. For a fun DIY project, try customizing a plain bag with crystals or sequins.

HOW TO STYLE IT
For Holly, this outfit represents a burst of color in an otherwise neutral wardrobe and signifies her carefree feelings of romance at this point in the film. The trick is to capture this put-together all-pink ensemble without looking too "matchy-matchy" or prim and proper. This is where flamboyant, fun accessories and the right attitude come in—don't take the outfit too seriously; wear it with a big smile and a party-ready vibe.

"Dress. Dress. Here we are. Bag, and a hat, too. There we are."

FUN FACT

In 2007, the pink dress from the movie sold for nearly $192,000 when auctioned at Christie's in New York—fetching more than six times the price expected by the auctioneers!

4 The Girl About Town

THE OUTFIT
In the scene where Holly and Paul head out to celebrate his selling a short story, Holly's been out partying all night—but that doesn't stop her from hitting the shops in style! Holly wears a funnel-neck, double-breasted vibrant orange wool coat designed by Givenchy, which was much copied after the film's release. She matches it with a black-and-white tweed boatneck belted dress, mink fur cloche, alligator heels, and a black crocodile tote bag with gold chain handles.

WHERE TO WEAR
A shopping trip, a lunch date

WHAT YOU'LL NEED
- Brightly colored funnel-neck coat, ideally with a '60s shape, which typically would have a belted waist, tulip-shaped bottom, and oversize buttons
- Neutral-colored fine-knit or tweed fitted dress to wear underneath
- Black kitten heels
- Oversize sunglasses
- Smart black Chanel-style handbag—patent, quilted, or crocodile effect, with chain detail

EXTRAS
A tall, black cloche, in felt or faux fur if possible. A beret could also work.

HOW TO STYLE IT
This outfit is all about the statement coat, as Holly knew and millions of later tribute designs confirmed. So focus on finding a good-quality topper in a thrift shop or online. If you can't find orange, red or pink will create a similar feel, as long as it's a vibrant, punchy shade. Single- or double-breasted will work, as will belted or unbelted. Oversize buttons are key for the vintage vibe, but you can easily replace them yourself on an otherwise perfect coat by picking up some buttons from a fabric shop or online. Most important, choose a coat you love and will want to wear again and again.

"Oh, I love New York!"

DONT
WALK

FUN FACT

The vibrant coat Holly wears in this scene, known for its iconic, almost fluorescent orange color, is made from a special Italian fabric known as *Panno Casentino*. The wool has been handwoven in the Casentino area of Tuscany since Roman times. You can visit the factory in the village where it's still made and even tour the Wool Museum, home to a replica of Holly's coat from the film.

5 Holly's Boudoir Chic

THE OUTFIT

As a girl about town, Holly Golightly lives a life that revolves around late nights and sleeping until lunchtime. This means she spends a fair amount of time in nightwear—something she pulls off with style thanks to her signature gamine charm. But her most memorable sleepwear look is the one in the scene where she meets Paul for the first time.

As a master of quick-change transformations, she speedily pulls on a men's formal white dress shirt before answering the door. The tailored piece has an old-fashioned stiff bib front while giving the impression of a casual men's nightshirt—all of which was carefully conceptualized by the film's costume supervisor, Edith Head.

Sleeping during the daylight hours means Holly has to wear an eye mask and earplugs to shut out the noise and glare from the busy Manhattan street below. Head skillfully transformed these functional items into objects of beauty—fashioned in iconic blue silk with gold embellishments and lilac tassels—creating instant must-have accessories coveted by generations since.

WHERE TO WEAR

Lounging around your shared apartment on weekends, or to a pajama party

WHAT YOU'LL NEED

· Boyfriend-shirt nightie: Wear an actual men's dress shirt, or take inspiration from the masculine shape by wearing a men's nightshirt or pajamas in crisp white cotton. Roll up the sleeves to the elbow for full effect.

· Tasseled earplugs: See DIY instructions on the next page.

· Silk eye mask: These are widely available at many stores or online retailers. Go for a light blue if you can, in order to best channel Holly Golightly. Some even have a similar elegant gold trim and embroidered eyelashes, as found on Holly's original mask.

· Ballet-style pink slippers: Like those Holly inexplicably finds in her fridge!

EXTRAS

A retro champagne glass to sip milk from Holly-style

HOW TO STYLE IT

The trick to looking stylish in nightwear, à la Holly, is to choose sharply tailored pieces and keep them well pressed and crisp. Ensure that your casual hair and natural-look makeup are on point rather than messy. The idea is to convince people you got out of bed looking this good—even though in reality it took some work. Wear an air of nonchalance, as if it's perfectly normal to be in your pajamas at 2 p.m.!

"Quel night!"

MAKE YOUR OWN TASSELED EARPLUGS

Follow these instructions to create your very own pair of Holly-inspired earplugs. Feel free to get creative and select earplugs and tassels in your favorite colors for a unique and personal twist.

WHAT YOU'LL NEED

- 1 pair of purple or pale blue earplugs (plastic or foam)
- 2 lilac or pale blue silky tassels (inexpensive options are found at fabric shops in the curtain section, where they are sold as rope ties)

Use a small dab of clear superglue to affix the round, closed-loop end of each tassel to the flat end of the earplug. Leave to dry for several hours before using. Then, voilà! You have a perfect pair of Holly Golightly–style earplugs.

Lightly Does It: An Accessory Master Class

Throughout *Breakfast at Tiffany's*, Holly demonstrates time and again the power of using the right accessories to dress up or down any outfit. Whether it's jewelry, hats, handbags, or shoes, she makes every item work and reuses each one again and again.

Here are some of her favorite multiuse items—and tips on how you can add them into your wardrobe too.

Statement Jewels

Not only does Holly have a vast array of tasteful costume pieces, but she also has some strong views on the subject of jewelry. "You could always tell what kind of a person a man thinks you are by the earrings he gives you. I must say, the mind reels," she tells Paul, while holding up an enormous sparkly crystal pair that are apparently too flashy, even for her.

STEAL HER STYLE

Holly's warnings aside, it's worth investing in several pieces of costume jewelry to add instant vintage glamour to any outfit. You can pick up pretty designs very reasonably from many clothing and accessory stores—or hunt through thrift stores for some eye-catching bargains. Pearl chokers, ideally multistrand, transform an outfit, as do long single strands, which you can knot jauntily or wrap around several times. As Holly demonstrates, pearl or crystal earrings are a fun and easy way to add sparkle. Seek out pieces with a retro Chanel or Givenchy vibe for the full Golightly look.

Embellished antique brooches are also fabulously versatile—pin one onto a choker to create a unique statement piece or attach one to a hair band. Tiaras are another Holly favorite, and these days moderately priced examples are easily found. As an alternative, jewel-encrusted headbands and hair combs can create a subtle but still sparkly feel. Keep a few statement accessories handy in your handbag, as a necklace and earrings quickly transform a work-appropriate black dress into a glamorous evening look for a last-minute invitation.

Shoe Stoppers

With the notable exception of some briefly glimpsed hot pink heels, Holly is seen wearing only two pairs of shoes in the entire film—a pair of black ballet flats and a pair of black alligator kitten heels. Yet these two versatile shapes see her through every style eventuality, from cocktail parties to impromptu shopping trips. This just goes to show that if you buy cleverly, you don't need to own racks of shoes to be chic—plus you'll be doing your bit for sustainable fashion in the process.

THE BALLET FLAT

It was Italian luxury footwear shoe designer Salvatore Ferragamo who first developed the ballet flat in the early '50s. The shoe quickly became a Hollywood favorite and is still popular today. The simple shape is just like a traditional ballet shoe, made from buttery soft leather but with a thicker sole and heel to cope with walking outdoors. Unusual for a flat shoe, its delicate design means it never looks frumpy, managing to successfully combine ultimate comfort with understated glamour. In the movie, Holly Golightly can be seen sporting a cute pointed-toe pair with cropped jeans in the "Moon River" scene and again, combined with capri pants, in the scene when she and Paul go out for an impromptu dinner.

STEAL HER STYLE

To model Holly's look, pair ballet flats with cropped pants, jeans, or a sundress. They smarten a casual look in lieu of sneakers and soften a smart look in place of heels. They're also great for looking chic where lots of walking is involved, such as shopping trips or traveling through airports. It's useful to own a couple of pairs in different colors for maximum wear. Black or nude leather are great neutrals that go with everything, while vibrant colors such as hot pink or bold prints like leopard or polka dots give edge to simple monochrome outfits.

THE KITTEN HEEL

When she's not in ballet flats, Holly is only ever seen in kitten heels. Perhaps the most wearable shoe height, this '60s favorite has a skinny mid- to low heel, usually $1\frac{1}{2}$ to $1\frac{3}{4}$ inches or less. But this style is about more than just height—what makes a shoe kitten-heeled is the heel's placement and its feminine shape. It has a slight curve and is inset from the back of the shoe. The best thing about these heels is they can be worn with just about any outfit, for those times when you want some height and chic without the drama and discomfort of a really high heel

STEAL HER STYLE

Kitten heels work during any season and with nearly any outfit. Closed-toe styles are great with dresses and smart long pants, while open toes work well with skirts and cropped pants during the spring and summer. The not-too-high heel makes them ideal for work or daywear. Those with pointed toes and slim heels look chicer and more sophisticated than those with rounded toes and chunky heels. The only thing to be careful about when wearing kitten heels is the length of your dress or pants, especially if you're on the petite side. Avoid anything that hits below the knee as this cut with these heels can make legs seem wider and you seem shorter.

Solid colors are more classic than patterns, but texture can add interest, as with the famous alligator shoes Paul hunts for under Holly's bed!

"Would you be a darling and look under the bed and see if you can find a pair of alligator shoes?"

Bags of Style

BLACK PATENT TOTE

Holly's favorite girl-about-town bag is a black patent croc-embossed tote with gold handles. This Chanel-inspired style goes with everything, and naturally she takes it everywhere.

A tote is a name given to any large and often unfastened bag with parallel handles on each side of its pouch. They tend to be made from a stiff, sturdy material, and Holly's tote is fashioned from shiny textured leather in a distinctive shape that is still a classic.

STEAL HER STYLE

Take your pick, from designers like Chanel to mid-price brands to ten-dollar knockoffs, any will add class to your outfit. Nearly every handbag brand still offers a version of this shape—many with textured or quilted finishes and chain details like Holly's. If you'd like a genuine '60s tote, you can find some great vintage bargains in thrift stores, online, or on handbag exchange websites. And if you'd prefer to steer clear of leather, look for vegan options.

THE CARPET BAG

In the scene where Holly comes home with Paul after a rather tipsy night out, she is carrying a large carpet bag with leather edging and handles, a Renaissance-style painting woven into the main fabric. The oversize carryall is clearly packed with many items, as Holly has to root around looking for her black coin purse to pay Paul.

A carpet bag tends to open at the top and is typically made from a woven fabric in the style of a vintage Oriental rug or tapestry. When it was first designed as a sturdy and attractive travel bag back in the 1800s, its fabric exterior was cheaper to come by than leather. Adding a relaxed daytime vibe to any outfit, the practical design holds more than most.

"Hand me my purse, darling."

STEAL HER STYLE

These bags are perfect for those long days out when you need a lot of stuff—cram in a scarf, makeup, sunglasses, a book, and even flat shoes for the walk home. Thankfully, carpet bags are still popular today and can be easily bought secondhand. Hunt for one similar to Holly's in thrift or consignment stores or online.

Use these pages for your own fashion notes.

"Darling . . . you're making me blush!"

Blush-Worthy Beauty

Throughout *Breakfast at Tiffany's*, Holly Golightly's makeup is understated and elegant. The smoky cat eye with winged eyeliner and false lashes paired with pale pink lips is a soft yet striking look that would come to define the early '60s. And this was a deliberate style choice by Wally Westmore, the legendary silver screen makeup artist. Holly was a very modern girl, Westmore understood, and he wanted her makeup to reflect that it was 1961, and a new decade in which fashion and makeup—and indeed culture—were being shaken up and pulled into an altogether fresher aesthetic direction.

This meant leaving behind much of the heavy glamour makeup from the previous two decades—thick powder, dark red lips, and tightly curled hair—in favor of a lighter touch. Sharp-eyed fans will notice that the older women in the cast, such as Paul's lady friend, still wear this more dated '50s-style makeup, a stark contrast to Holly's fresh-faced look.

Within this chapter are some practical ways you can take inspiration from Holly's iconic makeup, including how to update and adapt some of the film's most memorable looks, as well as the powder-room essentials every modern girl needs.

High Five:
Create Holly's Magic Makeup Moments

Evening Makeup That Still Looks Good the Next Morning

When we meet Holly in the film's opening scene, she's been out all night, but her makeup still looks perfect. Here's how you can re-create her classic elegant evening look—and give it some serious staying power.

ENDURING COVERAGE

For a flawless-looking complexion that will stay put all day (and night), first apply a lightweight skin primer to your face, leaving it for two minutes to sink in. Follow with a full-coverage, long-lasting foundation, applied with a foundation brush or cosmetic sponge. Choose an oval-shaped brush with soft and fine but densely packed bristles, and move in small circles for a poreless finish. Set with a light dusting of loose mineral powder.

PRETTY PINK CHEEKS

Holly's blush is a pretty, soft pink. For a long-lasting finish, use a finely milled mineral powder blush, applied with a medium-size slanted brush to the apples of your cheeks—the rounded part. Traditional advice is to smile to find the apples of your cheeks, but don't smile too much, as this encourages you to place the blush too low, which gives the illusion of a drooping face. Keep the color high on your cheekbones, and blend it out to the temples for a modern feel.

SULTRY CAT EYES

Apply a matte, pale cream-colored shadow all over your lid, stopping just below the brow line. This creates a base that will help your makeup last. Follow with a medium brown shadow on the lid, blended in with a soft brush. To create Holly's signature winged eyeliner, apply a gel liner right into the roots of your top lashes with a small angled brush. Create a cat eye by measuring just one brush length from the outer corner of your eye— the shape of your cat eye should be in the direction that would meet the end of your eyebrow if the line were to continue. Apply two coats of waterproof mascara for lovely lashes that will last all night.

BOLD BROWS

Take a fine, angled brush, and use small soft strokes to fill in your brows with a matte brow shadow—no pearl or shimmer. A taupe or medium brown works for redheads and blondes, but go a couple of shades darker if you're a brunette. The trick is to add depth and re-create Holly's thicker, natural brow shape without going too harsh and dark.

LIPS THAT WON'T QUIT

The color Holly wears here falls somewhere between a red and a coral, softer than a true red. Choose a long-lasting lipstick formula, and after lining your pout with a matching pencil to boost longevity, apply the lipstick with a brush for even, long-lasting color. After applying one coat, blot with a tissue, then apply a second coat. This will help ensure your lipstick stays put.

TOP TIP

Copy a professional makeup-artist trick, and set your entire face with a fine mist of water or setting spray (sold by many cosmetics brands) to ensure that everything stays in place all night. Hold the spray at least eight inches from your face to avoid saturating and disturbing your makeup.

Holly's Around-the-House Nude Makeup

Even when Holly's at home, and has just woken up, her face looks naturally flawless despite an apparent lack of makeup. But rest assured, she's had a little help—it's all about perfecting the no-makeup makeup look!

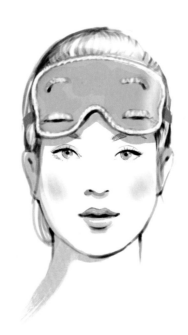

DRESSED-DOWN SKIN

Heavy foundation is a dead giveaway that your look isn't natural, so apply a light daytime serum to ward off dryness, and leave for five minutes to let it absorb into the skin. Then, using your fingers, apply a little tinted moisturizer or BB cream in a shade darker than your normal base for a warm, dewy finish. Cover any dark circles or other imperfections with a little concealer using a clean lip brush or concealer brush, and blend carefully. Resist the temptation to finish with powder.

ROSY CHEEKS

Choose a soft pink cream blush for a gorgeous, rose-kissed glow. Apply with your fingers to the apples of your cheeks, building up the color gradually.

MAGNIFIED EYES

Brush through your arches with a brow gel in a shade lighter than your brow color for a natural look. Use an eyeliner that matches your skin tone on your lower waterline. This helps create the illusion of larger eyes.

LUSH LASHES

Try a celebrity trick and visit a salon to have your lashes permed and tinted. This procedure lasts up to six weeks and gives you curled, dark lashes without mascara. It's the ultimate in "I woke up like this!" For a DIY version, buy an at-home eyelash tint, and use a classic lash curler, or choose a heated version for longer-lasting results.

KISSABLE LIPS

Complete the look with a barely there flesh-toned moisturizing lipstick for a natural-looking pout. Or simply use a clear lip balm.

TOP TIP

Don't have a heated eyelash curler? Before curling your lashes, hold a hairdryer over your curler for 20 seconds to warm it up—but be very careful not to allow hot metal to touch the delicate skin on your eyelids.

FUN FACT

British-born Wally Westmore, who created Holly's makeup looks, was one of six brothers, all of whom became notable film makeup artists. Wally served as the makeup department head at Paramount Studios for an impressive 41 years!

Golightly Evening Glamour

When Holly throws her party at home, her makeup is a master class in how to do all-out glamour without looking made up—a stark contrast to many of the other guests at the party, who wear bright red lips and dark eye shadow. Holly manages to look fresh-faced yet sophisticated with subtle pink lips and soft but still defined eyes. The good news is it's easy to pull off Holly's hostess look with her signature smoky cat eye and luscious false lashes using these expert tricks.

COMPLETE COVERAGE

Choose a full-coverage foundation with blurring qualities for nighttime perfection. Apply with a slightly damp blending sponge, making sure to press the foundation into the skin gently but firmly. Set with a little loose powder applied with a large, soft brush.

BEST LIGHT

Unless, like Holly, you are blessed with delicate bone structure, clever makeup can help you emphasize all the right features. Pick a creamy highlighter for extra definition, and apply with your ring finger to highlight your upper cheekbones, cupid's bow, and down the center of your nose—all the places light would naturally hit. Blend well with a soft makeup sponge.

SMOLDERING EYES

Pick a soft charcoal powder eye shadow to create Holly's nighttime party eyes. Use an eye shadow brush with soft bristles to add a wash of gray shadow onto the eyelid, focusing the product on the outer corners. Blend it with a clean blush to create a hazy look, and apply a little underneath each outer eye corner. Then take a black kohl pencil or liquid eyeliner, and draw along the lash line, stopping three quarters of the way along to slightly wing out the line and create a feline flick.

ULTIMATE LASHES

Holly loved her falsies, and they were a vital part of the signature '60s eye look. Select a natural-looking pair, without too much distracting drama, ideally slightly longer on the outer edges. Be sure to measure them against your natural lash line and cut them to fit before using. The trick for fuss-free application is to place a thin line of glue to the false lash strip and leave it for a minute to allow it to go tacky. This ensures it sticks properly and doesn't slide off. Then press it on as close to your natural lash roots as possible, following the natural line.

LOVELY LIPS

Holly's lipstick is a subtle mix of pink and peach. This creates a muted overall effect—after all, this look is all about the eyes. Choose a shade to suit your coloring with a soft, creamy finish.

TOP TIP

To remove falsies without damaging your natural lashes, soak a cotton swab with an oil-based eye makeup remover, and run it gently across the roots of the lashes a couple of times. This will help dislodge the glue so the false lashes slide off. Don't peel the lashes, or you may pull out some of your own lashes too!

Smart Girl About Town

Holly's day makeup is just as gorgeous as her evening looks, but it has a slightly lighter touch—perfect for a shopping trip like the day out around Manhattan she enjoys with Paul.

FRESH FINISH

For Holly's day look, a mid-coverage foundation or BB cream is ideal. You want a natural finish, but one that blurs out any blemishes. Buff it into the skin in a circular motion with a soft-bristled foundation brush.

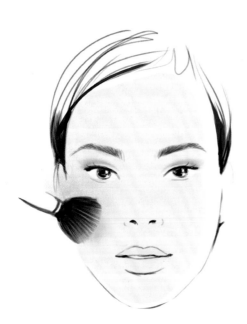

FLUSHED CHEEKS

Choose a peach-hued powder blush. Take a medium-size blush brush and lightly swirl it around in the color, tapping off any excess, then apply to the center of the apples of both cheeks. Use a circular motion to create that vintage flush.

"Oh, golly, darling. I did so want to impress you."

KITTEN EYES

The goal is to keep the eyes softer but still well-defined through the day. Apply a mink-brown soft shadow onto the eye crease and blend well. Then carefully apply liquid liner, using a subtler touch than for the night look—think more kitten than cat eye. Stay close to the upper lashes, and gently flick out at the outer corner.

LONG LASHES

Use an eyelash curler to open up your eyes, and apply two coats of dark brown mascara for a naturally long-lashed effect.

TOP TIP

If you want to add some Holly-style drama to your eyes without using a full set of false lashes, try a few individual lashes. You can buy them in varying lengths, and they can be applied to the outer corner of the eyes with normal lash glue for more natural definition.

PALE PINK LIPS

Daytime is all about the perfect pale pink lip. First, exfoliate using a dab of moisturizer and a soft, damp wash cloth. Rub in circular movements over the lips to gently remove any skin flakes that would otherwise show when a light color is applied. Line lips using a baby pink liner, and then apply a pale matte pink lipstick carefully with a lip brush. Blot with a tissue, and you're ready to go.

Pretty in Pink

When Holly goes out dressed head to toe in pink with her Brazilian beau José, her perky pink makeup perfectly matches.

PERFECT MATCH

Holly's complexion always looks the picture of perfection. The best way to get this finish is to make sure you find your perfect shade of foundation. Do this by applying a few shades to the side of your face—not the back of your hand—and check the colors in natural daylight. The shade that disappears is the right one. With a liquid foundation, dot directly onto the face and use fingers or a makeup sponge to blend. Cover dark circles and imperfections with concealer, and set your makeup with loose powder.

GOLDEN GLOW

For some evening party dazzle, apply golden liquid highlighter to help create the look of candlelit skin. Use sparingly along the top of the cheekbones, just below the outer corners of the brow bone, and along the center line of the nose. Apply soft pink cream blush onto the cheek apples, blending out to the temples.

'60S EYES

Cut-crease eye shadow was all the rage in the 1960s. A simple technique to achieve this vintage look today is to apply a light, neutral shadow all over the lid and brow bone, then a darker medium brown or gray shadow in the crease of the eye. This creates the appearance of large, defined eyes. Follow with liquid liner for a cat eye flick, layers of mascara, or false lashes if you prefer.

DEFINED BROWS

A small but firm blending brush is key to Holly's defined yet soft eyebrow look. Outline the edge of each eyebrow with a soft pencil in a color as close to your natural brow as possible. Be bold, but then soften with the brush to avoid your brows looking stark and severe.

HOT PINK LIPS

To create a well-defined cupid's bow like Holly's, use a medium pink pencil to line your upper lip just above your natural line. Then, using a lip brush, apply bright pink lipstick to the new shape, creating fuller, more defined party lips. Blot lips, and apply a second coat.

TOP TIP

After applying mascara, use an old, thoroughly cleaned mascara wand to carefully brush through every lash, helping to lift them and avoid clumping. Movie makeup artist Alberto De Rossi, who worked during Hollywood's golden age, famously separated each lash of the actresses he worked with, using a pin to create a voluminous, feathery look.

Five Makeup Essentials
for Every Powder Room

Always prepared and yet perpetually in a hurry, Holly keeps a spare lipstick, bottle of perfume, and handy mirror in her mail pigeonhole in the entrance hall of her apartment building, perfect for adding final touches as she rushes out the door. She also carries a full set of grooming goodies in her purse at all times for powder room visits and back-of-cab touch-ups.

A pretty makeup bag is worth investing in, but it needn't be a designer piece. You can upcycle a vintage-style purse: Take inspiration from the sequined clutch Holly carries on her date with José, and find a simple fabric envelope bag. Sew or glue reclaimed pearls around the V-shape seam on the closing flap for some retro glam. Whatever purse you go for, keep these Holly-inspired essentials inside it at all times.

Trusty Pink Lipstick

Holly never likes to be seen without a glossy pink pout, so she always has her lipstick on hand, enrobed in a pretty gold case. Opt for beautiful packaging for a hint of style every time you use it. This is where it's worth investing a little more money and going for one of the old-school French designer brands such as Guerlain, Yves Saint Laurent, or Christian Dior. All were around in the '60s, and many of their products still come in the same high-end glamorous gold casing.

Pressed Powder Mirror Compact

As Holly knows, every girl needs an excuse to pop to the powder room from time to time—even if it's just to escape an overly amorous suitor! Pressed powder in a stylish gold compact is a '60s classic that oozes sophistication. Find an ornate case you love, either new or secondhand. Then, select an inexpensive powder refill and slide it into the compact. *Et voilà!*

Mini Perfume Bottle with Old-Fashioned Bulb Atomizer

This will deliver instant French boudoir glamour. The scent Holly is seen spritzing herself with in her apartment hallway is Makila by Jean Patou, which was popular in the '60s but has since been discontinued. To achieve a similar look, source a genuine vintage or retro-inspired new bottle online and simply decant some of your favorite scent into it.

Vintage Tin of Breath Mints

Holly would never be caught without fresh breath. In this time period it was popular to carry a tin of breath mints at all times—or, for Parisian chic, rose- or violet-flavored sweets in an ornately decorated tub. If you can't find one pre-filled, shop for a pretty vintage tin or pillbox, and add your own mints.

Mini Cake Mascara

Holly's mascara in the film, which we see her apply when she's getting ready to visit Sing Sing prison, is a solid cake of pigment inside a tin, with a separate applicator brush, as all mascara was until the late 1950s, when Revlon debuted the first modern tube and wand. However, as more of us try to avoid plastic, this vintage approach is surging in popularity again, which means it should be relatively easy to source retro solid mascara in super-cute tins. Not only is it very easy to use—just wet the brush with water to apply—but it's also perfect for building up layers of mascara for dramatic eyes à la Holly. It can even double as eyeliner!

Find Your Perfect Pink Lipstick

After she is released from jail, Holly sits in the back of a yellow taxi faced with a breakup letter from José and insists on applying her signature pink lipstick before reading it. Makeup for Holly, as for many, is a suit of armor protecting her from the outside world.

To find your own perfect shade of pink, you need to know your skin's undertone. This subtle coloring affects which makeup hues make your face look bright and alive and which drain it. One easy way to determine your undertone is to look at the veins on the inside of your wrist. If they look blue or purple, you have a cool undertone; if they look greenish, you're warm. If you don't notice a color, you're probably neutral.

It takes a little work to test different shades, but it's worth it when you find your perfect pink lipstick to face the world.

IF YOUR UNDERTONE IS:

COOL

You look best in purple, black, emerald, bright blue, lavender, and pink. Aim for warmer, richer pink lipsticks.

WARM

You look best in olive green, brown, coral, orange, amber, yellow, and peach. Go for lipsticks with cooler true pinks and some blue in them.

NEUTRAL

Lucky you! You look great in almost any hue you choose. Explore whatever pink lipsticks strike your fancy.

"A girl can't read that sort of thing without her lipstick."

Skin Saviors

People with a social life as busy as Holly's need to look after their skin more than most. Late nights and too much champagne can indeed wreck a complexion. But with these tips, everyone can maintain gorgeous, glowing skin—no matter how late they're out!

"There are certain shades of limelight that can wreck a girl's complexion."

Quick Makeup Removal

After a late night, removing your makeup before bed is the last thing you feel like doing. But leave it on, and you could end up with irritated skin, blocked pores, and blemishes. Avoid beauty disasters by investing in a few items to make things quick and easy.

MAKEUP REMOVAL WIPES

Ensure they're biodegradable to help protect the planet, and choose an option designed for sensitive skin and free from irritating astringents. Keep them handy on your nightstand.

ALL-IN-ONE EYE AND FACE WATERPROOF MAKEUP REMOVER AND WASHABLE COTTON ROUNDS

It's worth keeping these on hand if you wear long-lasting mascara, which requires something with a bit more oomph to sweep away. Reusable cotton rounds reduce waste, which is kinder to the environment than disposables.

FACIAL MICROFIBER SPONGE OR CLOTH

Holly could have done with these clever inventions, which require only a splash of water to remove most types of cosmetics. They are super convenient and help you save money on cleansing products. Do remember to moisturize after use.

Wake Up Beautiful

Using the right overnight skin-care products with nourishing ingredients helps you wake up with Holly's radiant glow—even after a late night.

TRY A NIGHT OIL

For a boost of radiance, night oils can be your best friend. They penetrate the skin, providing a great vehicle for active ingredients such as vitamins A and E. Or choose one containing lavender oil—this super ingredient can soothe skin irritation and help promote a good night's sleep.

INVEST IN A MULTITASKING NIGHT CREAM

There's nothing like the luxurious feeling of slathering on a super-hydrating cream before bed. To boost your glow while you sleep, try applying a multitasking product that not only hydrates but also exfoliates for a fresher morning face. Look for one that contains AHAs (alpha hydroxy acids), glycolic acid, or low-dose retinol—all of which work to slough off dead skin cells as you sleep.

PUT ON A FACE MASK

Overnight masks are a great way to treat your skin and give it a little extra attention. The skin undergoes intense cellular repair while we sleep, so it can be more receptive to products at this time. Simply cleanse, slather on a layer of the mask, and then snooze. Buy one or make your own DIY version by mixing the naturally skin-nourishing ingredients on the next page.

TOP TIP

To protect your pillowcase from your overnight face mask, place a clean hand towel on top of the pillow to add a layer between your skin and pillow.

DIY OVERNIGHT FACE MASK

This simple mask is a quick and easy way to
nourish your skin while you sleep with three
simple ingredients that can be sourced from
your local grocery store.

YIELD: 1 MASK

- 1 tablespoon honey
- 1 teaspoon avocado oil
- 1 teaspoon heavy cream

In a small bowl, whisk together the honey,
avocado oil, and heavy cream until fully
combined, then gently rub the mixture into
the skin with your fingertips. Try to sleep
on your back, at least for the first part of the
night, to ensure that the mask is absorbed
into the skin rather than rubbed off on your
pillowcase! Gently wash away the mask in
the morning.

SLEEP IN PLUMPING UNDER-EYE PATCHES

A great recent invention is the under-eye patch infused with moisturizing ingredients—perfect before a night out. Better still, apply it before bed and leave on overnight for a more potent effect. Choose patches that contain hyaluronic acid, which deeply hydrates and plumps the skin, and you'll wake up with fresh-looking eyes.

LAYER ON HOMEMADE LIP BALM

Blend together half a teaspoon of coconut oil with one drop of vanilla essential oil, and rub it into your lips. You'll wake up with a soft and flake-free pout. Make a larger amount and keep it in a small glass tub with a screw-top lid next to your bed. It will last up to six months.

"How do I look?"

— HOLLY GOLIGHTLY

"Very good. I must say I'm amazed."

—PAUL VARJAK

SKIN INGREDIENTS TO AVOID

If you have sensitive skin, check the ingredients list before you buy cosmetics and try to avoid products that contain common skin irritants:

FRAGRANCE OR PERFUME

Used to make beauty products smell nice, scent is, unfortunately, the most common skin irritant.

SODIUM LAURYL SULFATE

This widely used foaming agent can strip away the skin's natural protective layer of oil, which can lead to dryness and sore skin.

PARABENS

Many people are sensitive to these common preservatives, which are widely used in skin products to increase their shelf life.

TEA TREE OR CITRUS ESSENTIAL OILS

Often used to target breakouts or oily skin, but many sensitive skins find these oils too harsh, and they can trigger allergies.

MINERAL OIL AND SILICONE

Both these ingredients are used to help make products smoother and glide more easily over the skin, but for sensitive or blemish-prone skin types they can block pores, triggering breakouts and irritation.

LANOLIN

Derived from sheep's wool, this natural moisturizer is often used in beauty creams but can trigger an allergic skin rash in many.

CHEMICAL SUNSCREENS

Used to give a product UV protection, sun filters such as oxybenzone and avobenzone are a common cause of contact dermatitis—a bumpy irritated skin rash.

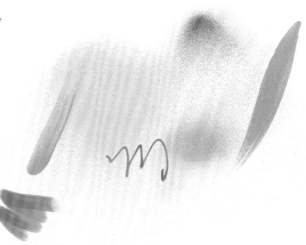

Inside-Out Beauty

"We are what we eat," goes the saying, and scientific research reveals that consuming the right nutrients can boost skin health. You may not have a Hollywood makeup artist at your disposal, but eat plenty of skin-friendly superfoods each week and you can achieve glowing Golightly skin.

BLUEBERRIES

These berries help boost the strength of collagen fibers—the building blocks of skin that keep it plump and springy— thanks to their high concentration of anthocyanins: plant nutrients that give them their bright blue color.

SWEET POTATOES

These vegetables contain disease-fighting compounds called carotenoids that give them their distinctive color and which research has found can help protect the skin from sun damage and keep it healthy and glowing. Just one sweet potato contains 200 percent of your recommended beta-carotene, an important carotenoid that the body converts into skin-boosting vitamin A.

ALMONDS

These nuts are packed with vitamin E, a vital skin nutrient that helps heal scars and protect against sun damage. (Please note that almonds do not act as an SPF.)

CARROTS

Carrots are high in the vitamin A precursor beta-carotene, which has been found to prevent the overproduction of cells in the skin's outer layer. That means fewer flaky dead cells that can leave skin looking dull and block pores.

SALMON

As well as being one of the most potent sources of anti-inflammatory omega-3 fatty acids, salmon also contains dimethylaminoethanol (DMAE), a nutrient that protects cell membranes.

TURMERIC

The active antioxidant in this culinary herb, curcumin, has been shown to be a highly effective anti-inflammatory and is therefore great for happy, healthy skin.

AVOCADO

This salad and toast favorite is full of monounsaturated fatty acids, which have been found to help hydrate skin from within and also protect it from sun damage and premature wrinkles.

LIVE YOGURT

As well as being a good source of skin-strengthening protein, yogurt contains probiotics, "friendly" bacteria which encourage a healthy digestive system— something multiple studies have linked to clearer skin.

GLOW-LIGHTLY SMOOTHIE

Start the day with this delicious
drink, packed with super-nutrients for
radiant skin.

YIELD: APPROXIMATELY 16 OUNCES

- 1 cup almond milk
- 1 tablespoon live yogurt
- Handful of blueberries
- Half a banana
- Half an avocado
- 1 teaspoon honey
- 2 ice cubes (optional)

Combine the almond milk, yogurt,
blueberries, banana, avocado, and honey
in a blender or with a hand blender,
adding ice if you prefer your smoothie
cold. Serve in a tall glass.

FOODS TO AVOID

To keep your skin in tip-top condition and as smooth
as Holly's, avoid junk food, which research has found
exacerbates skin problems. Fried food such as burgers and
breaded chicken, white carbohydrates such as bread and
cakes, sugary soft drinks, too much alcohol, and artificial
sweeteners are just a few of the unhealthy foods that are
harmful for your skin.

Body Care:
How to Get Holly's Silky-Smooth Skin

Easy Exfoliation

By the early '60s, trips to the salon or spa were part of life for glamorous girls about town like Holly. One popular salon treatment involved scrubbing the skin with a textured washcloth or loofah, slathering it with lotion, and then wrapping the body tightly in layers of cloth and resting that way for an hour. This was thought to improve skin texture, fight cellulite, and even help with slimming. Thankfully, there are easier ways to buff and soften skin these days.

BODY BRUSHING

Dry body brushing has been used for centuries to exfoliate and remove dead skin. The vigorous action is also thought to boost circulation and stimulate the lymphatic system to help the body eliminate toxins. Invest in a round wooden brush with soft bristles, and brush in long upward strokes from the bottom of your body toward your heart. Do this daily before a bath or shower.

BODY SCRUB

Another great natural way to slough off rough, dead skin, a body scrub can be used in the shower or bath.

CARDAMOM & BROWN SUGAR BODY SCRUB

Try this luxurious recipe for an affordable but luxe DIY scrub.

YIELD: APPROXIMATELY 12.5 OUNCES

- Seeds from 5 cardamom pods
- 1 cup organic coconut oil
- 1 tablespoon sweet almond oil
- ½ teaspoon vanilla essential oil
- 6 tablespoons coarse brown sugar

Using a mortar and pestle, crush your cardamom seeds into a fine texture. Then add the coconut oil, sweet almond oil, and vanilla essential oil, and mix until creamy. Finally, stir in the brown sugar, and transfer the mixture to a jar. It's ready to use and will keep at room temperature for up to six months.

Bathing Beauty

Back when Holly was strolling the streets of New York, a daily soak in the tub was an important part of most beauty routines (showers were less common). Indeed, at her cocktail party, Holly is first seen wearing a bath towel—styled to look stunning, it has to be said. This spur-of-the-moment gown is never explained on film, but Holly is in fact late to her own party after lazing in the bath. The bath scene, sadly, was cut from the final edit of *Breakfast at Tiffany's*, but it was featured in a September 1961 *Life* magazine pictorial shortly before the film was released.

BATH OIL

As Holly definitely knew, soaking in a warm bath is the perfect time for some self-care. Sprinkle a few drops of scented bath oil into the water to help you relax away the day's stress and moisturize skin. For ultimate luxury, decant yours into an old-fashioned 1950s glass jar or bottle to bring some vintage glamour into your bathroom.

"Simply do not ask me what this is all about. Parce que je ne sais pas, mes chers."

BODY LOTION

Shea butter and cocoa butter were all the rage in this era, and these natural moisturizing ingredients can be found in a host of organic beauty products today. Shea butter is packed with antioxidants such as vitamin E, as well as polyphenols and phytonutrients. These ingredients make shea butter an anti-inflammatory, which is why it works so well at moisturizing and soothing all types of skin. Cocoa butter is also incredibly moisturizing, creating a barrier on your skin to help lock in moisture. Cocoa butter also contains high amounts of antioxidants to help mop up free radicals (rogue molecules that attack our cells), which can otherwise inflict damage and age your skin.

HOLLY'S WHIPPED ROSE BODY BUTTER

Create a '60s-inspired moisturizing cream Holly would have loved.

YIELD: APPROXIMATELY 16.5 OUNCES

- 1 cup shea butter
- 1 cup coconut oil
- 3 to 5 drops rose essential oil

Place shea butter, coconut oil, and rose essential oil in a blender, and mix until completely smooth.

Pour mixture into a mixing bowl, and place in the refrigerator to cool until it solidifies.

Using a stand mixer or hand mixer with the whisk attachment, whisk until it takes on a whipped consistency similar to whipped cream. Spoon the whipped butter into a glass tub or jar with a lid. Store in a cool place such as a cupboard for up to 6 months.

Use these pages for your own makeup notes.

"I haven't had my hair done, but I'm happy, really happy. It probably shows!"

Hollywood Hair

There's little doubt that Holly Golightly's distinctive hair plays a role in her iconic style and is a key reason why her look still captivates us today. Most famous of course is the updo to trump *all* updos—a beehive with a French chignon back, resplendent with a diamond-and-pearl tiara. This all-out glamour is still the ultimate party princess look some six decades after the character graced the big screen.

The 1960s saw huge changes in hair fashion, not least the introduction of highlighting, or lightening strands all over the head to create a color contrast. Indeed, when *Breakfast at Tiffany's* was released, in 1961, highlights were the new must-have style for many young women, and sure enough, Holly's hair is subtly streaked with lighter tones.

However, '60s hairstyles were perhaps more notable for what they left behind. Gone are the short, tight curls, the victory rolls that became popular in the 1940s, and pin curls typical of the 1950s. Rather than going to sleep in rollers, Holly represents a significant shift into a more relaxed vibe. Big hair was still very much expected in the evening, however, which is where the beehive comes in—an iconic look Holly truly makes her own.

In this chapter, you'll learn how to get Holly's hero hair, adapting it for a more modern feel, with four easy-to-follow tutorials. Plus, we look at hair-care tricks that will lend you Holly's on-screen shine.

Tease Me, Baby!

How to Create Root Volume Without Damage

The art of teasing hair at the roots is the key to Holly's most memorable hairstyles, and indeed to many '60s-inspired looks. This combing technique is a great way to add volume to your hair, but it's important to do it properly so you don't end up damaging your locks and causing spilt ends.

Back when Holly styled her beehive, a fine-toothed comb was always used. Today, hair-care companies make a teasing brush, a flat, thin tool with densely packed bristles and a long, thin, pointed handle that's able to tease more hair at a time than a normal comb and helps create more tension against the hair, so your lift will hold longer. However, a humble comb worked well enough for Holly and will do the trick if that's all you have on hand.

Hair won't hold its shape for long without help, so it's important to use products designed to give extra texture and lift, such as dry shampoo or texturizing

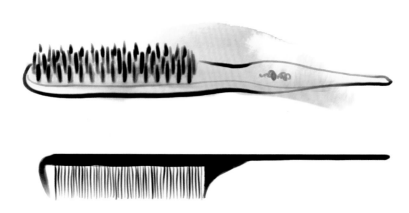

spray. Comb each section through before teasing so you don't end up with a tangled mess at the top of your head. Then divide the hair into manageable sections, and use your brush or comb to gently but firmly push the hair back toward the scalp, right down to the roots.

Using one fluid motion for each stroke will help you achieve a uniform effect rather than an uneven look. Start at the crown with a section no wider than three inches. Work back and down the sides, repeating the same technique on each section. When you've achieved your desired shape and height, smooth out the top section to cover the teasing, secure the hair ends, and spritz with a little hair spray.

TOP TIP

When it comes to brushing out your teased style, start at the ends and work your way up to the crown, easing out tangles as you go. Don't brush hard from the top down or you will damage your hair.

Rock a Baby Bee

Holly's elegant beehive is the original it-girl hairstyle. And like any true classic, it looks as fabulous today as it did 60 years ago. This smaller, softer version is an easy everyday look that also feels perfectly modern.

GET SECTIONED

Start with clean, center-parted hair, and divide it into four sections, secured with clips. The first two sections should be about two to three inches wide and start from the top of the ear and go to the middle part—these will be pulled forward to hang in front of your face. The third and fourth sections should be much larger and divided horizontally across the back of the head and clipped at the nape of your neck.

USE A DRY SHAMPOO

Lift the top horizontal section of hair at the back of your head, and spray a little dry shampoo at the roots (see our recipe on page 82 to make your own). Then, gently massage through the hair, concentrating at the scalp, distributing the powder evenly so it becomes invisible. This will add some volume to your mini beehive, giving it a strong base.

TEASING: GOLIGHTLY DOES IT

The more you tease, the bigger your beehive. So, since we're creating a softer look here, take a small amount of hair from the top horizontal section—four to five inches—and use a teasing brush or fine comb to lightly tease the hair down to the root and create a bit of height.

BRUSH HAIR INTO PLACE

Smooth over the teased section with a soft brush to ensure there are no frizzy strands and you're left with a small dome shape.

SECURE THE HIVE

Gather the teased section of hair together, and roll and tuck the hair ends under neatly, securing in place with bobby pins that match your hair color.

FORM A BACK BUN

Now twirl the lower section of the hair, and then use your fingers to twist the hair into a fairly neat but casual low bun at the base of your beehive. Bobby-pin it into place, making sure the hair from the back sections is tucked in. But remember: It doesn't have to be perfect for this daytime look—a few loose tendrils are good, too.

ADD FINISHING TOUCHES

For an even softer look, leave the two front sections of your hair loose to frame your face, using a curling iron to create soft waves, or pin them loosely behind the ears if you prefer. Once you're happy, spritz with a soft hold spray, which allows some movement so it doesn't look too structured or set.

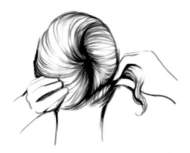

TOP TIP

Team this hairstyle with a pared-back beauty look and simple day jewelry to keep it fresh and modern.

Take Your Updo to New Heights

It's time to experiment with extra height and a Holly-style tiara! This special-occasion look is of course modeled after Holly's hair in the film's opening scene, when the camera lovingly lingers on the perfect chignon of her neatly coiled beehive.

GET PREPPED

A high beehive works best on hair that hasn't been washed for a few days and that is shoulder-length or longer. Start by sectioning off your hair, leaving two small one- to two-inch pieces free at the front to frame your face. Divide the back horizontally into two larger sections, and clip the lower section into a ponytail. Because we're going for a bigger beehive here, make the top section larger, using about a third more hair than the lower section.

GET TEASING

Take the top section of hair and hold it upward vertically to tease it. Keep going all over the front section of your hair and around the side of the section to create a good amount of height at the roots.

FUN FACT

High, conical hair, fondly nicknamed the beehive for its resemblance to one of nature's great wonders, is thought to have been created by famous Chicago hairdresser Margaret Vinci Heldt in 1960, one year before *Breakfast at Tiffany's* was released. The look quickly became popular with stars of the day, from girl group the Ronettes to First Lady Jacqueline Kennedy.

CREATE YOUR BOUFFANT

Take the teased front section, gathering it together from behind, and push it forward until you get the beehive bouffant shape and height you desire. Bigger is better here! Then secure with a hair band or slide.

ROLL IT UP

Next, take the bottom section of hair, unclip it, and spray with some styling spray and brush through to stop flyaways and make the hair easier to work with. Then twist the ends inward and under to the left, creating a roll, or chignon. Start your roll at the nape of the neck, and work gradually upward to the base of the beehive. Secure the roll with evenly spaced bobby pins (pushing them into the roll fold so they're invisible) until all the ends are neatly tucked in and your roll is secure. Use a hand mirror to check the back, and make sure you fix the top of the roll so it covers the band or slide holding the top section in place.

SMOOTH IT OUT

Carefully use a soft brush to very lightly neaten all around the front and back, ensuring you don't pull out any strands or disturb the shape. Be sure not to put too much pressure on the brush, as this will flatten all that volume you've worked so hard to achieve!

CROWNING GLORY

It's tiara time! Fix your chosen headpiece around the front of the beehive, being careful to position any jewels in the center. Attach with bobby pins to secure in place. Finally, spray liberally with firm-hold hair spray, avoiding the tiara where possible so you don't dull its sparkle!

TOP
TIP

Not into the full tiara look? For a more subtle variation, try crystal or pearl hair slides or combs added at the side or back for just a touch of bling. Or wear a jewel-embellished headband on top for a knowing nod to Holly's sparkly vibe.

Make Your Own Tiara

Follow these easy steps to create your own Holly-inspired tiara, perfect for wearing in your beehive hairstyle.

WHAT YOU'LL NEED

- Thin silver headband
- 1 piece of paper
- Pencil or pen
- Roll of 16-gauge soft silver wire
- Scissors or wire cutters
- Flat pliers
- Decorative crystal beads in various sizes and shapes (at least one 2-inch bead for the tiara center)
- Hot-glue gun

DRAW THE TEMPLATE

Holding the headband at the bottom of a piece of paper for sizing, draw a template for your tiara design. Check out photos of the tiara Holly wears in the opening scene for inspiration. A simple three-teardrop design, comprising one large central teardrop with two smaller ones on each side, works well.

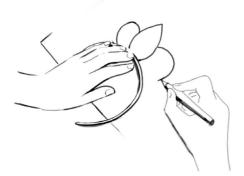

SHAPE THE WIRE

Using the template underneath, take the wire and trace the shape you drew, using the pliers to help mold the wire into the shape you want. Once you have the desired shape, leave about two inches of extra wire on each end, and use wire cutters to cut the wire.

ADD THE BEADS

After each curve on the wire is
shaped, take a selection of beads
and thread them onto the wire
and all around the design. Leave
two inches of wire at each end for
affixing onto the headband later.
Take your time and make sure the
wire is smooth and the shapes
are symmetrical. Fix each bead in
place with hot glue.

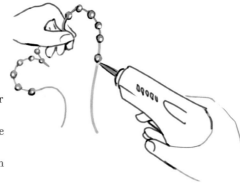

ATTACH THE HEADBAND

Glue the design onto the headband, wrapping the
spare wire on either end around the headband a
few times with the pliers for extra security.

MAKE THE ACCENTS

Cut three straight pieces of wire, one for
each teardrop height, but with a spare two
inches at the bottom and one inch at the
top. Then string a mixture of crystal beads
onto each wire, with the largest ones in the
center and smaller ones at either side.

AFFIX THE ACCENTS

Fix one beaded wire into the center of each teardrop,
wrapping them around the headband at the base and around
the point of the teardrop at the top, fixing in place with the
pliers. Voilà—your own sparkly tiara.

TOP TIP

To go for a more film-
inspired look, glue the
beaded tiara wires
to a hair comb that
can be slid into your
beehive hairstyle.

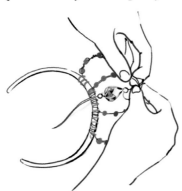

Holly's French Pigtails

When Holly heads into Manhattan wearing pants and a sweater for a spontaneous dinner with Paul, she's certain she's finally about to marry José, a very wealthy Brazilian politician. Her more relaxed hairstyle reflects her lighter mood. Here's how to pull off this chic low-pigtails look, with a little height on top for a perfect dressed-down style.

PREPARE YOUR LOCKS

Wash your hair the day before creating this hairdo, as your natural oils will help create a bit of hold, so the style doesn't slip out. Brush hair through so it's tangle-free.

FRONT IT UP

Grab some hair from the top center section of your head, leaving out bangs if you have them. If you don't have bangs, leave a three-inch-wide section on both sides of your face at the front.

EASY TEASY

Tease the center section with a teasing brush or a fine-toothed comb, then section the piece of hair just below it, going no further down your head than halfway, and lightly tease that section, too. This will help the top section stay in place.

PIN IT

Use a long hair slide to pin this underneath section in place, covering it with the very top section of teased hair. Grab a little hair from the sides to help cover if necessary. Tuck in all the ends, and secure with bobby pins. Spritz with hair spray to secure.

CURLY GIRL

Use a curling iron to add soft twirls, section by section, to all the lower hair that remains loose. This adds volume and neatens the final effect.

PARTING THE WAVES

Take all the hair that's still down, and create a neat center part, dividing it into two low pigtails. Secure with hair ties that match your hair color, keeping the bunches low at the nape of the neck.

TOP TIP

To vary the look, try braiding your pigtails. Two-strand or fishtail braids tend to look more sophisticated and less schoolgirl than the classic three-strand variety.

Half-Up, Half-Down Hair

Not everyone can look as effortlessly glamorous as a half-awake Holly when she first answers the door to Paul, but you can channel some of her boudoir bed-head style with this easy around-the-house look.

PREP CLEAN HAIR

Start with clean hair before you create this softer look. Apply some hair oil throughout your locks. This will give you some much-needed "slip" as you comb and tease. Remember, a little goes a long way!

SECTION IT OFF

Leave two three- to four-inch sections of hair down at the front on each side of your face and lift up the middle, back section.

ADD HEIGHT

Using a teasing brush or comb, lightly tease the middle section of hair upward, so that some height is created. Continue to lightly tease the sections to the left and right of the middle section, forming the shape of your half-up, half-down mini beehive.

TIDY UP

Use a soft brush to gently smooth out the teased section and tame any frizz, being careful not to disturb the height.

TWIST AND PIN

Using both hands, bring the middle and side sections together toward the middle, adjusting until you're happy with the shape and height. Hold all three sections, and twist the back of your hair together to create your mini bouffant. Then, pin your twisted strands together with bobby pins that match your hair color, pushing them into the twist to hide them. Finish with some hair spray.

STRAIGHTEN UP

Use a flat iron to smooth out and slightly curl under the ends of the hair length that's left down. Gently brush through for a silky finish.

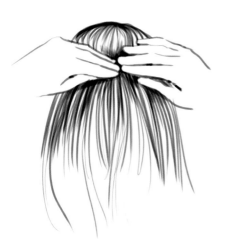

TOP TIP

To add retro vibes, track down a hair wrap, silk scarf, or hair scarf in a funky '50s-style pattern. Wear it wrapped around the top section and under the back, similar to how Holly does when she sings "Moon River" on her fire escape.

Healthy Hair Care

With salon highlights and daily heat and hair spray, Holly's locks would have needed plenty of care and attention to stay shiny, smooth, and ready for her next night on the town. Here's how to care for your own hardworking hair so it looks great from dusk until dawn.

Holly's Home Hairstyling Kit

- Hair spray to keep your beehive in place all day
- Hair protection spray to prevent heat damage from styling tools
- Heated hair rollers
- Hair tongs
- Hair straightener
- Large rounded-barrel hairbrush for blow-drying
- Blow-dryer (retro look if possible!)

"It's useful being top banana in the shock department."

Wash the Night Out of Your Hair

When using styling products regularly, it's important to shampoo often, but try to avoid washing your hair every day or you'll risk stripping away too much of the natural oil that hair follicles produce to protect it. When you do wash, choose a gentle, chemical-free product to lift away impurities. Take care not to use too much; you only need a teaspoon or so. Excess shampoo causes the hair follicles to swell, which gives hair a dry appearance and makes the scalp overproduce oil to replace what's been removed, leaving the roots greasy.

The best practice is to follow shampoo with a light, nourishing conditioner, combed through hair with a wide-tooth comb. But make sure you completely rinse it out, as any residue will leave hair dull. Apply conditioner only about midway down—not to your roots—or hair may look oily and limp.

MAKE YOUR OWN DRY SHAMPOO

It's easier than you think, and it really does work! Holly would have loved this idea, because it's perfect if you've been out all night and don't have time to wash your hair the next morning. It absorbs oil at the roots, and adds a bit of body and a fresh scent. Plus, it doubles as a useful styling product, adding volume and grip, making it ideal for teasing hair and creating beehives.

DIY DRY SHAMPOO

Try whipping up a batch of this easy dry shampoo to show your locks some love in between washes.

YIELD: 4 TO 5 APPLICATIONS

- 2 tablespoons cornstarch
- To match your color, add 1 teaspoon of one of the following:
  - Blond: arrowroot
  - Red: cinnamon
  - Brown: cocoa powder
  - Black: charcoal powder
- 1 to 2 drops lavender essential oil

In a small glass container, combine cornstarch with arrowroot, cinnamon, cocoa powder, or charcoal, and mix with a small spatula until well combined. Add lavender essential oil, and mix well again.

Dust a small amount onto your hair roots using a large makeup powder brush. Leave for 5 minutes to absorb excess oil, then brush out with a hairbrush. Store leftovers in a glass container with a screw-top lid. It will keep for up to six months.

Do Some Deep Conditioning

Using a rich moisturizing hair treatment or hair mask at least once a week is extremely helpful in keeping frequently styled tresses healthy. Prices can range from a few dollars right up to a hundred, so choose wisely and base your treatment on beneficial ingredients rather than brand names or packaging. Key ingredients to look for that help repair and restore moisture to dry hair include argan oil, avocado oil, babassu oil, pro-keratin, and vitamin B5. If you're looking for a budget-friendly natural option, make your own with our handy DIY recipe.

COCONUT & ROSEMARY HAIR MASK

Try using this simple and fragrant mask on your hair once a week for ultimate Golightly locks.

YIELD: 1 MASK

- 1 tablespoon coconut oil
- 3 drops rosemary essential oil

Mix the ingredients together in a small bowl until fully combined.

Massage into damp hair, and leave on for at least an hour. Wrap your head in plastic wrap or a warm towel to help the oil penetrate the hair shafts. Be sure to shampoo thoroughly afterward to remove excess oil and ensure that you get all the conditioning benefits without leaving your locks looking lank!

WHY IT WORKS

Coconut oil penetrates the hair shaft and protects against protein loss. Meanwhile, rosemary oil is a natural antifungal that has been found to be effective at preventing dandruff and soothing an itchy scalp.

"*I've got to do something about the way I look!*"

Classic Male Grooming

In *Breakfast at Tiffany's*, Paul Varjak—and most of the other male characters—are always impeccably groomed. Paul has neat, sleek, well-cut hair and is always clean-shaven, in keeping with the styles of that time. Styles may have changed since the '60s, but there has been a definite renewed interest in male grooming in recent years.

Young men are discovering the pleasures and advantages of old-school barbering for their beard and hair, with a new breed of retro barbers having sprung up, offering wet shaves, shampoos, and short back and sides haircuts, much like the places Paul probably visited.

A visit to the barber has become a pampering experience for many urbanite men, but you don't need to visit a pricey establishment to enjoy the benefits of a wet shave. It's something you can do at home or, indeed, ask a friend or partner to help you try.

DIY Wet Shave

START WITH THE RIGHT EQUIPMENT

Enjoying an old-school shave means investing in a proper shaving brush and soap. The best brush is one with good-quality bristles. Badger bristles are traditional, but for a cruelty-free option, there are some great styles with soft nylon, vegan-friendly bristles that are more than capable of lathering up a decent pre-shave foam.

The soap should be moisturizing but also able to work up a lather. For the full experience, go for a straight razor (in steady and trained hands). A classic stainless-steel razor works best for those without any formal training. Wet a washcloth with hot water, and hold it against your face for a minute to soften the hairs and open pores.

Then wet the brush, and swirl it in the soap (in a shaving scuttle or a mug) before applying it to your face in brisk, circular movements to build a thick, creamy lather ready for the blade. Applying in circular motions helps to separate the hairs from the skin.

SHAVE IT OFF!

Now perform one gentle pass over the face with the razor, going from top to bottom, with the grain, not against. Do not push down. Let the razor's weight do the work. For the neck, continue to shave with the grain, this time from bottom to top. Rinse and repeat as necessary.

Wet your washcloth again, this time with cold water, and wipe off any excess soap. This will also close the pores. Then moisturize, and apply a little aftershave. This helps reduce redness and irritation and prevent those annoying razor bumps.

Get Paul Varjak's Sleek Hairstyle

Paul's hair is as cool and collected as his character—it stays put throughout the entire movie, even during the downpour of the final scene!

In fact, Paul's side sweep with a mini quiff brings together two classic looks of the day. In the late 1950s, the likes of Elvis Presley and James Dean had made the quiff the ultimate rock and roll hairstyle, while a neat side part was ubiquitous for the older professional man.

As an urban literary type, Paul works a combination of both styles to create an altogether sophisticated, modern look. He retains the sleekness of the conservative side part but sneaks in some subtle rebellion with a mini quiff, held in place by pomade, which also supplies his hair with the trademark shiny finish.

Of course, these days, this classic men's style looks fashionable regardless of gender. All you need is a quick lesson in retro combing and parting techniques.

"Anyone who ever gave you confidence, you owe them a lot."

WAX LYRICAL

Rub a little pomade or other styling cream between your palms, and smooth the product into the sides and top of your hair.

PICK A SIDE

You'll need a medium-size comb to exaggerate your natural side part and achieve a sharp-looking finish. Use it to comb your hair to the side, creating a neat part.

MAKE A MINI QUIFF

Comb the top section away from the part, so there is a clean divide, then lift and shape your bangs to the side and upward. If you want some extra lift, use a small-barrel hairbrush behind the quiff, wrapping the hair up and over it from the roots. Then blast with a blow-dryer for 30 seconds on hot, followed by 30 seconds on cool to set.

COMB THROUGH

For a polished look, smooth and neaten everywhere with the comb. Or, for a slightly more natural result, rough it up a little with your hands. Now you're good to go!

TOP TIP

If shine is not your thing, opt for a styling paste, which is translucent and matte, so your hair still looks and feels like hair. This ensures that your style stays in place without looking oily.

Feed Your Hair From Within

Eating the right foods can help keep your crowning glory in tip-top shape.
The following nutritious foods help support healthy hair.

EGGS

These are a great source of protein and biotin, two nutrients that may promote hair growth. Eating adequate protein is important, because hair follicles are made mostly of protein. A lack of protein in the diet has been associated with hair loss.

NUTS

These snack favorites are packed with nutrients like vitamins E and B, zinc, and essential fatty acids, all of which may promote hair growth and are linked to many other health benefits.

SALMON

In addition to fabulous skin benefits, fatty fish like salmon, fresh tuna, and mackerel are great sources of omega-3 fatty acids, which have been linked to improved hair growth and thicker, healthier hair.

SEEDS

Like nuts, seeds are rich in vitamin E and other nutrients that may promote hair growth and boost shine. Some seeds, such as flaxseed, also contain omega-3s, which have been linked to improved hair growth.

SPINACH

This leafy green veggie is loaded with folate, iron, and vitamins A and C, which may promote hair growth. A deficiency in these nutrients has been linked to hair loss and may cause dull hair.

SWEET PEPPERS

Colorful and crunchy, these are a rich source of vitamins A and C, two nutrients that help ensure hair stays healthy and may aid hair growth.

FOODS TO AVOID

As with the rest of your body, to keep hair in good health, avoid too much fried or processed foods, and cut down on sugar and alcohol.

SHINE ON
BREAKFAST SMOOTHIE

Start the day with this yummy smoothie, packed with nutrients to promote gorgeous hair.

YIELD: APPROXIMATELY 16 OUNCES

- 1 cup cashew nut milk
- 1 tablespoon flaxseed
- 2 handfuls fresh spinach leaves
- 1 Medjool date, pitted
- 2 ice cubes (optional)

Blend the cashew milk, flaxseed, spinach, and date in a blender or with a hand blender, adding ice if you prefer your smoothies cold. Serve in a tall glass.

"Come on, darling. Let's eat."

Use these pages for your own hairstyling notes.

"If I could find a real-life place that made me feel like Tiffany's, then I'd buy some furniture and give the cat a name."

"I'll Take Manhattan" Dream Decor

Her chic clothes may have made her a fashion icon, but it's Holly Golightly's hip apartment that launched a million Manhattan fantasies. As the former small-town Texas girl proved, New York is the place for a carefree twenty-something to reinvent him or herself—a city of endless possibilities.

Holly lives in a small rented apartment in one of the much-coveted brownstones on Manhattan's Upper East Side. But back in 1961, it was still considered daring for a young woman to live alone, albeit with a "poor no-name slob" cat for company. In lifestyle, then, as in so many other ways, Holly could be considered a trailblazer in possession of a modern, independent spirit, pursuing the kind of self-reliant path many young people aspire to today.

As a love letter to New York, *Breakfast at Tiffany's* beautifully re-creates the rhythms and textures of city life, among them the bustling streets and vibrant bars. And yet most of the film takes place inside the four walls of Holly's small and often chaotic apartment.

The apartment is a perfect reflection of the lead character herself. The decorating decisions may seem eccentric, but as a seasoned party thrower, Holly knows just what to display and what to hide. Her open shelving has conversation pieces on it such as books and the odd bottle of champagne, while her telephone is kept quiet inside a suitcase.

The color palette is predominantly white, which helps the small space feel airy, but much like Holly would dress up a favorite frock, her apartment is accessorized with pops of color such as the hot pink sofa cushions and zebra-print rug. It's the singular quirky character touches that we love and covet the most.

In this chapter, explore how to invite some of Holly's eclectic interior design into your own home.

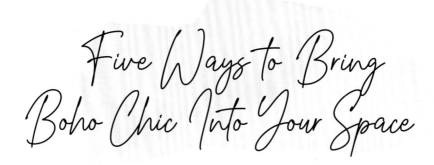

Five Ways to Bring Boho Chic Into Your Space

GRAB AN ANIMAL-PRINT RUG

The zebra rug in Holly's living room is a striking splash of pattern in an otherwise minimalist space. The black-and-white design is bold and showcases the monochrome trend that would come to be a popular motif in the 1960s.

Used playfully like this, animal-print accessories add texture and pattern, and lend an exotic and traveled feel to a room, making them a great tool for layering. They also add warmth and glamour. This is one style trick that's easy to steal from Holly, with faux zebra rugs widely available in home stores and online, many for as little as twenty dollars.

USE VINTAGE SUITCASES AS STORAGE

Pretty white leather luggage can be seen stacked artfully in Holly's apartment next to the entry door. For Holly, this prominent position might represent her carefree nature—ready to escape at a moment's notice—but it's also a stylish idea for hiding clutter, especially in apartments where space is at a premium and it's tough to fit larger storage furniture (or indeed store suitcases).

Displayed luggage also makes a nice accent piece that hints to visitors that you love to travel. Look for retro tan, cream, or white suitcases with leather strap details, and buy a few in descending sizes to stack. Several luggage brands make beautiful new vintage-inspired bags, but they can be pretty expensive. Alternatively, look for secondhand bargains online and in thrift stores—battered is better here for added character.

REVIVE A RETRO RECORD PLAYER

Holly has a gorgeous cream-and-tan record player that comes in its own fold-up leather box with handles, giving her a stylish but portable way to play her vinyl and ensure that her parties swing. The '60s were the golden age for record players, when they became a must-have in every home thanks to the invention of the automatic high-fidelity turntable. Brands such as Dansette and Champion made popular versions you can still find secondhand today, and which can often be restored to working order.

With the recent resurgence in popularity of vinyl, many manufacturers now produce vintage-style leather-box record players, so this is one retro trend that is right back in fashion. The benefit of these newer players is that they look the part but also come loaded with modern features and technology, such as Bluetooth connectivity. These reproductions tend to be a fraction of the cost of buying a genuine antique and restoring it.

PICK UP AN OLD-STYLE TELEPHONE

Dress up your entryway or living area with a retro rotary phone like the one Holly keeps in a suitcase—it may not be very practical, but it is symbolic of her kooky charm. These classic designs are still lusted after today and add a touch of nostalgic charm to a space. Buy a genuine antique phone from a vintage shop, or pick up a reasonably priced replica with push buttons and other modern features.

HANG A DECORATIVE BIRDCAGE

Holly has a birdcage in her living room containing a fake parrot that has a cameo role during her party. In the '60s, it was fashionable to use Victorian-style ornamental cages as decorations, and it's a trend that's still popular today. When placed on a shelf or hung from a ceiling, they add a touch of bohemian Victoriana, showing visitors your quirky side. Pick up an inexpensive one from a home goods store or thrift shop and leave it empty or transform it into a display for a vining plant. Another option is to put small tea lights or a single pillar candle into the cage, creating a soft evening glow.

"I'll never let anyone put me in a cage."

MOVIE MOTIF *The Birdcage*

This seemingly frivolous piece of decor becomes more meaningful when free-spirited Holly tells Paul, "I'll never let anyone put me in a cage." The cage in her home represents the fear she has of being trapped and the self-sufficiency she craves. But the motif comes full circle during the final taxi scene, when Paul points out that an obsession with freedom to the point of refusing love can become a trap in itself. "Well, baby, you're already in that cage," he tells her. "You built it yourself ... it's wherever you go. Because no matter where you run, you just end up running into yourself."

Upcycling the Golightly Way

As her beatnik apartment proves, you don't need money to have style. Holly was into recycling before it became fashionable. She wears an elegantly draped sheet as a makeshift party dress, fashions tables out of apple crates, her suitcases double as side tables, and her couch is an upcycled bathtub. Here are some ways you can repurpose items to create statement pieces just like Holly did.

Create a Rolltop Sofa

Holly's unique lounge seat is made by sawing an old Victorian-style rolltop, claw-foot bathtub in half. The bathtub couch has been a much-coveted and pricey piece ever since, and it's something you can make yourself. But be warned, this is not a project for the faint of heart, so you might want to skip it if DIY is not your thing. It's a big undertaking, but if you're creatively inclined and love a challenge, the results are more than worth the effort.

WHAT YOU'LL NEED

- Old-style claw-foot bathtub
- Bathtub cleanser
- Angle grinder with sanding disc attachment
- Mask
- Safety goggles
- Thick work gloves
- Tarps
- Sandblaster
- Replacement claw feet and bolts, if needed
- Paintbrush
- Can of enamel primer
- Can of epoxy or acrylic paint in white, cream, or pale gray
- Can of acrylic paint in gold or black, for tub feet

- Piece of upholstery fabric large enough to cover foam on both sides
- Iron
- Roll of tracing paper
- Pencil
- Sheet of plywood, as thin as possible, cut to fit your seat template (see page 102)
- Fabric adhesive spray
- Piece of 2- to 3-inch-thick foam padding for seat cushion, a few inches longer and wider than your bathtub (available from fabric stores or online)
- Electric kitchen knife or fabric scissors
- Staple gun and ¼-inch staples
- Brightly colored throw pillows

TOP
TIP

Be sure to cover your workspace appropriately. You don't want to drip primer or paint on your floors. This project is best done with help and outdoors, as bathtubs are heavy and difficult to maneuver by yourself.

FIND A TUB

Hunt in salvage yards or online. You'll be amazed how many are sold for just a few dollars. Don't worry if it still has the taps in place—Holly's did! Give the tub a thorough cleaning. Try to remove stains with a gentle but abrasive bath cleanser. This might leave you with a good enough finish, or you can paint it later.

SLICE IS NICE

If you've never used an angle grinder, kindly ask a handy friend or relative who knows how to use it safely to remove one of the tub's long side panels. Be sure to cut away enough to make a comfortable seat, but not too much, as you'll need all four legs to still be firmly attached to the bottom. Bear in mind, the average rolltop bath has a depth of around thirty-one inches, while the average sofa depth starts at about thirty-one inches—so you really don't want to cut away any of the seat depth, just the side panel. If you don't know anyone who could help you, a local handyman should be able to do this for a reasonable fee. Call around to find the best price—a little research goes a long way here.

CHEAT IT

If you want to get the look of Holly's sofa without quite so much work, shop around for a mid-century secondhand sofa with a quilted, rounded back and curled, retro-looking arms—the curvier the sofa shape the better—and ideally one with shaped feet you can paint gold. Choose a white, cream, or pale gray color, or cover it with a throw in this shade. Then jazz it up with vivid pink and purple throw pillows.

GET SANDING

Be sure to wear a mask, thick work gloves, and proper safety goggles to protect yourself for this step. Do this project outdoors to keep yourself and your home safe. Lay down a tarp under the tub. Use a sandblaster to sand down the exterior of the tub. Be sure to sand all the newly exposed, cut edges, so no sharp areas are left. If you don't have access to a sandblaster, you can hire someone to help with this step or look into tool sharing options in your community. If you hire someone to make the cut for you, ask them to sand down the edge for you as well. If you're doing it yourself, add a sanding disc attachment to the angle grinder to smooth out the sharp edge.

NOTE: Do not sand the tub interior as this will damage its porcelain glaze.

REPLACE THE CLAW FEET

Depending on the quality of your salvaged tub, the claw feet and bolts may need to be replaced. Source replacements online, and install according to their instructions.

PRIME AND PAINT

This is another step best done outdoors. Prime the exterior—and interior if you're painting it—with enamel primer, and leave to dry overnight. Then paint both the interior and exterior using the epoxy or acrylic paint. A standard paintbrush is fine to use and you will probably need two coats, so allow drying time in between. Go with white, cream, or pale gray for a Holly Golightly '60s feel. Paint the claw feet in contrasting black or gold.

MAKE A COMFY NO-SEW SEAT CUSHION

Iron the fabric for the cushion. Using tracing paper and pencil, make an exact template of your seat, and ask your local DIY store to cut a piece of their thinnest plywood to fit it. Outdoors, spray one side of the board with adhesive, and stick the foam onto it. Cut away excess foam with an electric knife or fabric scissors. Lay out your ironed fabric and place the foam-covered board, foam side down, in the center. When your fabric is straight, starting with the long, straight edge, wrap it over and pull taut. Staple that side to the board, pulling it taut as you go. You might want a friend to help here, to hold the fabric tight while you staple. Space the staples evenly every couple of inches or so. Continue around the curves of the cushion, paying extra attention at the corners to make sure the fabric doesn't bunch up, until it's all covered smoothly and stapled in place. Turn over the seat cushion and slot it onto your bathtub sofa.

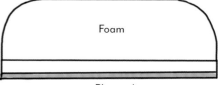

Glue foam to plywood and trim excess foam

Foam

Plywood

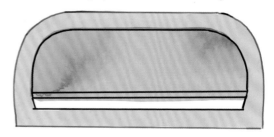

Place onto back side of fabric with the plywood side facing up and the foam side facing down.

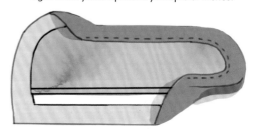

Pull fabric up and over the plywood, holding it tight while you staple every couple of inches.

FINAL TOUCHES

Style with a few scattered throw pillows of your choice—hot pink like Holly's or any black-and-white monochrome print.

Paint Everything White!

Holly's apartment is almost completely white, giving it a crisp modern feel. Painting a space white is a really affordable but effective way to spruce it up. There's a reason property developers often style everything in white when they put a property on the market to sell—it immediately looks stylish and expensive!

You can go for brilliant white, soft white, or off-white. When you're happy with your color choice, paint all the walls (checking with your landlord first, if you have one). Ask friends for help, and make it a paint party. Be sure to use any necessary floor coverings, and allow for proper ventilation.

If you want to paint your kitchen cupboard doors white, like Holly's, look for a specialist paint that has a wipeable finish.

Thinking about painting your furniture white? For a shabby chic feel, it's a good idea to use chalk paint, a favorite among upcyclers, that can be bought from your local paint store. Chalk paint is very easy to use because it doesn't have to be applied perfectly but gives a beautiful, soft, vintage-looking finish.

Create a Coffee Table

Holly uses two upturned wooden apple crates as a casual coffee table. Go one step further and make an even more stylish design by nailing four old crates together for a unique piece that will last.

WHAT YOU'LL NEED

- Tarps for floor covering
- 4 crates
- Sanding paper
- 1 can of wood stain
- Paintbrush
- 1 large piece of plywood
- Saw
- Wood nails or screws and a hammer
- 4 furniture caster wheels and screws
- Screwdriver or electric drill

SOURCE WOODEN CRATES

Fruit and vegetables, as well as quality wine, are still often shipped in wooden crates, so it's worth asking around local grocery stores for four unwanted crates for free. Any style is fine, but you do need to make sure they are all the same size so they will fit together neatly. You can also buy empty wooden crates online at pretty affordable rates.

SAND AND PREPARE

Remove jagged edges or loose wood, and smooth with sandpaper. Wipe with a clean damp cloth to remove any wood dust.

PROTECT THE WOOD

For this step, be sure to allow for proper ventilation, and cover floors with tarps. It's also best done outdoors. Use two coats of wood stain in your chosen color to help protect the wood and give a nice, smooth finish. Make sure to allow ample time for each coat to dry between applications. Leave to dry completely overnight.

ARRANGE CRATES ON THE TABLE BASE

Instead of using the bottom of the crates as the tabletop, you will be using the long sides. This will give you handy storage spaces on the outside of your table to keep magazines, records, or other trinkets. Lay the crates vertically on the long sides back to back to form a two-by-two rectangular base so the openings face outward. Make sure there are no gaps on the outside—although there will be a square hole in the middle because of how the crates tessellate on their sides. Cut the plywood to the size of the combined crates. If you don't have tools for this, measure the size you need and ask your local hardware store to cut a piece to size for you. Nail the crates in place onto the base, and screw or nail the crates to each other for stability.

FIX THE CASTERS

Turn the table upside down, and screw one caster wheel onto each of the outer corners of the table base with a screwdriver or electric drill. Be sure these go through the plywood base and into the crate. Return the table right side up.

FILL IN THE CENTER HOLE

Decide what to do with the square-shaped hole in the center of the table. Possible solutions include filling it with smooth, decorative pebbles and sitting a potted plant or candle on top.

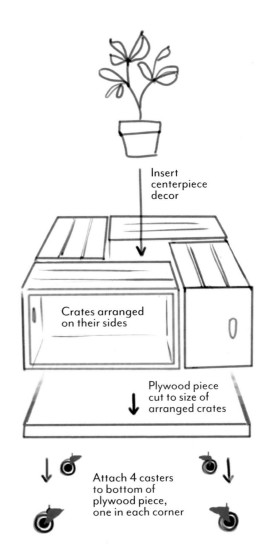

Insert centerpiece decor

Crates arranged on their sides

Plywood piece cut to size of arranged crates

Attach 4 casters to bottom of plywood piece, one in each corner

Thrift Shopping Made Easy

Probably the easiest and most affordable way to give your home a *Breakfast at Tiffany's* makeover is to hunt for preloved period bargains in secondhand shops and thrift stores. Of course, we don't see Holly hunting for used furniture in the film, but she clearly loves shopping, and her apartment is full of interesting pieces you could pick up only by looking in unusual places.

And it really doesn't matter what you find. Anything that speaks to you personally will help create the kind of eclectic 1960s boho charm you're cultivating here. Being open-minded and creative are the first steps toward curating a beautifully decorated, retro-inspired home without spending lots of money.

The good news is the global trend toward more sustainable shopping means secondhand furniture and home decor are more popular than ever. As a result, there are even more thrift shops and flea markets to scour for vintage bargains that have plenty of life left. Not only can great quality pieces be found for low prices, but secondhand shopping means you're reducing waste, keeping goods out of landfills, and often donating to a worthwhile charity.

Shopping secondhand is a stylish choice. Mixing a few thrift-store finds with modern pieces of furniture creates depth and adds an element of the unexpected—just the kind of vibe Holly's apartment had back in 1961. And mixing in newly sourced vintage touches with your favorite pieces keeps a room feeling fresh, interesting, and balanced.

If you're new to the art of thrift shopping, it takes a bit of time and effort to find the best pieces. The rewards, however, outweigh the challenges, and by following some of these go-to thrifting tips, you will be able to style your home with vintage items for fabulously low prices.

GO OFTEN

Secondhand stores often get new inventory every day, so check back often. Pieces that are rare or random tend to disappear quickly. The store itself needs to source the items—or have them donated—so if you get to know the staff, ask them to look out for items you're after and hold them for you.

SEARCH FAR AND WIDE

It's a good idea to shop at stores in different areas to give you a better chance of finding unique treasures. The types of items that are donated to a store are dependent upon the area it's in, which can work in different ways. Sometimes wealthier areas have more valuable thrift-store goodies. Of course, thrift stores in those zip codes tend to be popular with dedicated bargain hunters, and you might find that the store charges higher prices because it's in a higher-end area. The key is to get to know stores in different parts of town to give you a feel for where you have the best luck finding hidden gems.

CHECK ONLINE

Try internet searches to find thrift and secondhand stores near you. Thethriftshopper.com is a handy site that works as a national thrift-store directory. Simply enter your zip code and state, and you get a list of thrift shops in your area. It also includes the store's hours, distance from you, and reviews. You might be surprised just how many in your neighborhood you hadn't spotted before.

TAKE A LIST

If you're not sure what to look for, take a *Breakfast at Tiffany's* hit list featuring some of the items discussed in this chapter. Or keep an ongoing thrift-store wish list handy on your phone. This can help focus and streamline your shopping trip, so you don't get distracted by bargains you don't really need.

DITCH THE URGE TO MATCH

Don't be discouraged if you can't find complete sets of furniture or matching accessories. If Holly saw an individual piece she loved, she would have grabbed it—and your home will be personalized and eclectic when you've channeled some of her spontaneous spirit.

"A present for $10 or under, that I'll accept."

LOOK PAST A BIT OF DAMAGE

Holly's apartment is proof she can think creatively and see a second life in everyday objects. Anything with a decent build and foundation can be made over or upcycled, so try to visualize how something might look once you've given it a little TLC. Look for items that can be easily transformed—for instance, wooden furniture can be sanded down and varnished or painted. A lamp base that rocks great retro vibes can get a new shade. The picture in a frame may be unfortunate, but the frame can be painted and used to house a piece of artwork or a photograph you love.

TEST ELECTRONICS BEFORE BUYING

If you're buying items such as lamps or old record players, check that they work first. A nonworking item isn't necessarily a complete no-go if you love its retro look, but you'll want to factor in the price of repairs if you want it working again.

BE LOYAL

Many thrift shops have loyalty programs you can take advantage of by signing up with your email for reminders about special sale days or coupons for cash off on specific days.

TAKE ALONG YOUR OWN UNWANTED ITEMS

It's a really good idea to clear out before starting any home improvement projects. This will give you a clean slate to see which spaces you want to fill and what might work in them. Plus, making space in your home is important before adding more items, to avoid accumulating clutter. Donating to your local thrift shop is a good way to give back to a store you appreciate. It helps boost its income and keep it going, as it survives on donated goods.

"Did I tell you how divinely and utterly happy I am?"

Five Key Furniture Items to Hunt Down

Listed here are a few quintessential *Breakfast at Tiffany's* pieces to look out for. Grab them inexpensively, and then fix them up yourself to add your own personal flair.

Wrought Iron Headboard

Holly has a charming black scroll metal bed frame, and this classic style is one of the easiest ways to add vintage glamour to your bedroom. A new iron bed can be pretty spendy, not to mention difficult to transport and assemble. A much easier solution is to hunt for a headboard panel. Anything wrought iron with curls and swirls works well here. Check salvage or metal scrapyards, or purchase a new, lightweight version inexpensively from a home store or online. Most of these come in silver, but you can easily spray it black with some metal or vinyl spray paint if you want the true Holly look.

Room Divider

Holly has several room dividers in her apartment. Not only do they look pretty, but they are wonderful for small spaces, as they can section rooms off for different uses or create added privacy. Look for an old wood-paneled one which can be painted, or one with frosted glass panels that you can stencil pretty transfers onto. For example, Holly's wooden bathroom screen divider has a cherry blossom design printed across the glass. Many online stores have a wide variety of transfers with '60s-inspired designs.

Vintage Dressing Table

A classic dressing table creates the ultimate in vintage bedroom glamour. Holly has a stunning version that displays her vast array of perfume bottles, jewelry, and makeup. Find an old wooden dressing table with a typical 1950s or 1960s shape. Take Holly's table for inspiration, or do an internet search to get a feel for shapes from the time period. Seek out one that comes complete with its own vanity mirror and stool. It doesn't matter if it's battered and scratched, as long as it has a good solid base. Then put your own style spin on it by sanding it down and painting it yourself. For true Holly chic, go for a vintage off-white shade.

Rocking Chair

Holly sits and knits in a beautiful rocking chair while she prepares for what she thinks will be her new life in Brazil, married to José. Classic wooden rocking chairs have a timeless appeal and add a touch of folksy nostalgia and whimsy to a room. Look for one that's worn but structurally safe, so you can just sand it down and repaint it in your chosen shade. White or another pale hue will give you a true Holly feel, but you could go vibrant for a pop of color here.

Leaner Mirror

A large ornate full-length mirror is
essential for a party girl like Holly to
check over her chosen outfit. Oozing
bohemian chic, a leaner mirror like
Holly's looks beautiful standing on
a brushed wooden floor. Look for
one with lovely carved edges that can
be—you guessed it!—sanded down and
painted. For a touch of extra glam, try
silver or gold paint.

*"Isn't it wonderful? You see what
I mean, how nothing bad could
happen to you in a place like this?"*

Holly's Finishing Touches

It's the personal flourishes that make a stylish space feel like a true home. Holly's quirky apartment never feels like a showroom—it feels lived-in and has character, a reflection of the singular personality that has poured so many hours into it. Of course, that's not to say these aren't items that would also grace your space. Here are some of the pieces that lend Holly's apartment its unique vibe, many of which you may want to add to your own shopping list.

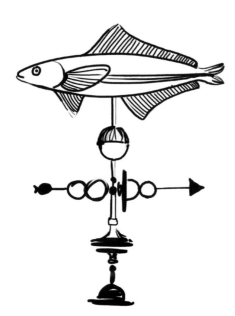

Weather Vane

Holly inexplicably has a large golden weather vane as an ornament by her front door, perhaps a nod to the suspicious "weather reports" she delivers to crime boss Sally Tomato when she visits him each week in Sing Sing prison. Whatever the story behind it, the weather vane perfectly demonstrates how a pretty but completely incongruous object adds immediate interest to a room.

Acoustic Guitar

The small wooden guitar Holly plays when she sings "Moon River" is a Harmony Stella. Hunt for any acoustic model from a thrift shop—the older the better. However, old guitars can warp and the wood can rot, so if you want to play the instrument, be sure it's in good enough shape. If you're not musically inclined, it can simply be hung on a wall for decoration. Although, for Holly, being able to play and sing helped to enchant Paul, so it might be worth investing in a few lessons!

Retro Glassware

Holly's home bar is a showcase for pretty glasses, and finding vintage glassware couldn't be easier. Thrift stores tend to have a good assortment of drinkware. Stock up on mix-and-match champagne bowl glasses, martini glasses, and cut-glass whiskey tumblers, and you'll be ready for your next party. Display them on open shelves in your kitchen or living room.

Vintage Perfume Bottles

Holly's dressing table is filled with perfume bottles in all shapes and sizes, and they add a gorgeous touch to any boudoir. Hunt in thrift stores and online for some genuine 1950s and 1960s fragrance bottles, and group two or three together for vintage glamour.

Pops of Color

Ever the style chameleon, when Holly gets together with José, her apartment takes on a very colorful feel with bright touches dotted around. The vibrant plants in pots, paper flower garlands, vintage Brazil posters, and vividly painted wooden bowls and salad tossers she uses to prepare a meal for Paul are all new touches. These bold colors look great against a white backdrop and are easy to find in thrift stores.

"It's a beautiful typewriter."

—HOLLY GOLIGHTLY

"Of course. It writes nothing but sensitive, intensely felt, promising prose."

—PAUL VARJAK

Crisp White Bed Linen

Despite her relaxed attitude toward most things, Holly's bed linen always looks fresh, crisp, and bright white—a girl needs a clean and warm place for her beauty sleep, after all! The trick is to buy the highest thread-count cotton you can afford (hunt for sale bargains at big department stores) for that luxury hotel feel, and wash using a little whitener to keep the fabric bright. For true boudoir chic, iron the linens well before putting them on the bed—the results are worth the effort.

Old-Fashioned Typewriter

You can pick up a secondhand typewriter like Paul's affordably to give your home a vintage literary appeal. Who knows? It may even help you write "sensitive, intensely felt, promising prose." Just make sure there's a ribbon in it!

Glittering Chandelier

While the chandelier seen in *Breakfast at Tiffany's* isn't in Holly's apartment, the way she gazes at it wistfully and her apparent love of rhinestone jewelry suggests she would have loved to have one in her own living space. And a chandelier would certainly have fit in perfectly with her overall boho vibe. These days, stunning replica chandeliers suiting most budgets can be purchased from home stores. Thrift stores and antique flea markets are also a great option for a genuine vintage bargain.

FUN FACT

The real New York City brownstone townhouse, located at 169 East Seventy-First Street on Manhattan's affluent Upper East Side, featured as Holly's home in *Breakfast at Tiffany's* sold for $7.4 million in 2015. Its iconic stoop, front doors, and architectural accents are immediately recognizable even today, although the green-and-white striped awnings over the building's windows in the film are no longer there.

Finding Your Own Happy Place

One of *Breakfast at Tiffany's* overarching themes concerns finding the place that, when life feels overwhelming or too sad, has the power to soothe your spirits. The idea of finding our own happy place is something most of us can relate to and is worth putting some time and effort into as an important part of self-care.

Seven Ways to Make Your Home Your Happy Place

Holly may have had to travel elsewhere to find her little place of calm, but there's no reason your own home can't become your ideal retreat.

DISPLAY YOUR MEMORIES

Remembering good times and loved ones is an instant mood booster, so put your favorite memories on display. These can be framed photographs or meaningful objects, such as shells from a favorite beach vacation. Anything you cherish that makes you smile will help lift your mood next time you feel low.

SPEND ON ITEMS THAT SPARK JOY

They don't have to be expensive, but choose furniture, artwork, and other decorations that truly capture your personal taste and interests, to help make your space feel your own.

LET THE NATURAL LIGHT IN

Holly's apartment is airy, but many homes lack natural light, which not only connects us to the world outdoors but is also essential to our body's internal clock. The circadian rhythms balance our sleep and wake cycles and control our moods. So position furniture near windows, open your curtains and blinds, reflect natural light with the help of strategically placed mirrors, and let the sunshine in to create a happy vibe and kick the gloom out of your room.

"I don't want to own anything until I find a place where me and things go together. I'm not sure where that is but I know what it is like. It's like Tiffany's."

KEEP IT CLEAN AND CLUTTER-FREE

Mess can trigger stress, so keep on top of tidying—even Holly's apartment is organized chaos! Having a clean, ordered space will help you create a sanctuary and place of calm to come home to. Kicking off with a decluttering session is a good idea. Recycle or donate anything that's no longer essential.

MAKE PRECIOUS MEMORIES

A recently released study from Harvard University carried out over 75 years suggests that the secret to human happiness is the formation of strong bonds with family and friends. So make your space somewhere loved ones can come together for special moments. A dinner table or a large cozy sofa will help create good times right now and happy memories for later.

GET A PET!

If you have the time, space, financial ability, and desire to safely look after one, then make like Holly and rescue an unwanted cat—or dog—from a shelter. Owning a pet increases your chances of being happy and successful, according to a study by OnePoll, which found that pet owners are more likely to be married, have a child, earn a degree, and find a perfect job. Having a close bond with a pet has also been found to boost natural feel-good biochemicals in our bodies such as endorphins and oxytocin, which make owners feel calmer and happier.

"Didn't I tell you that this was a wonderful place?"

GO GREEN-THUMBED

Holly's apartment doesn't have any indoor plants until later in the movie, when she's feeling happier and engaged to José. Then we see a huge number appear in her front room. And she had the right idea here. Many research studies have demonstrated that surrounding oneself with nature can help reduce stress and boost mood. Houseplants are great for helping purify the air—good choices include English ivy, peace lilies, and ferns.

Use these pages for your own decorating notes.

Golightly Entertaining

When Holly invites Paul for drinks at her apartment to apologize for storming out on him the night before, it turns out those drinks include dozens of other guests, music, and dancing. Holly Golightly, we soon discover, knows how to throw a wild party. A colorful cast of hip and stylish people pack into her tiny home to mingle, flirt, and generally create enough noise for the gathering to end—as some might argue all the best parties do—with the police being called by the neighbors.

A ball from start to sudden finish, it's little wonder the party scene in *Breakfast at Tiffany's* has become one of the most famous screen soirees of all time. With so much teeming life on show, every time you watch it, you find something new to notice or relate to. For instance, many of us can empathize with the female guest who starts the night out laughing raucously only to end it sobbing inconsolably. Or maybe you've known someone who, like Holly's friend Mag Wildwood, passes out unceremoniously on the floor after one drink too many. Or perhaps it's Paul you feel the most affinity with—out of your element but still enjoying people-watching from the sidelines.

Even if you prefer your parties on the smaller side, anyone who loves a good get-together can pick up some tips and tricks from the ultimate hostess, Holly. With this in mind, these easy-to-follow guides will help you throw three *Breakfast at Tiffany's*–inspired bashes. Whether it's chic cocktails at home, a pampering pajama party for your best friends, or a swanky champagne brunch, we've covered every detail to ensure that your special event has the kind of pizzazz Holly herself would love.

Throwing Parties in Small Spaces

Holly Golightly's apartment was about the size of a large shoebox, but she didn't let that stop her from throwing a swinging party for a big crowd. Tight spaces are a logistical problem for many of us, especially those living in city apartments like Holly's. Thankfully, chic entertaining in a tiny flat is entirely possible and can even add to the atmosphere, as the film's crowded bash proves. All you need is a bit of thought, planning, and preparation to ensure success in even the smallest space.

DECIDE GUEST NUMBERS

The number of people invited influences the type of party you can throw, so be realistic about how many you can accommodate. If you want high numbers, it will need to be an open party with finger food. If you're happy to invite just a select few and you have a reasonable-size dining table, then a dinner party will work, and floor space won't be an issue. The following tips cover how to make larger gatherings work with limited room.

MAKE FRIENDS WITH YOUR NEIGHBORS

If you're planning a party that may get loud or large, make sure you extend an invitation to anyone who shares a wall (or floor or ceiling) with you. Even if you've never met your neighbors, this courtesy will help keep the peace. As Holly discovered in the film, upsetting a neighbor with party noise can result in their complaining or even calling the police! And if your neighbors do show up, you might actually make new friends.

"And I always heard people in New York never get to know their neighbors."

—PAUL VARJAK

GO FOR A REVOLVING-DOOR TIME FRAME

Rather than fixing a short time period, starting a party early and ending it late can be the best way to allow the maximum number of guests to visit over the course of the evening without ever becoming overcrowded. For example, if you suggest guests arrive anytime between 5 p.m. and 9 p.m., they can choose to have a cocktail with you before heading off to another event or to show up after dinner. Although it makes for a longer time commitment as host, a staggered start will help spread out arrivals and departures and should ensure that you get to talk to as many guests as possible.

HAVE A PRE-PARTY DECLUTTER

Make some room for the party. Try to begin your cleaning process a week before the event to prevent the stress of doing it all on the day of the party. View it as an opportunity to think about what you actually need in your life and what you can recycle or donate. Hide unnecessary furniture and fragile items in a space that will be closed off for the party, such as your bedroom or home office.

But don't stress over what you can't change. Some items just can't be moved. In this case, have fun with them. Decorate or hang fairy lights on them and make it part of the party theme!

MULTIPURPOSE FURNITURE

When planning a party in a small space, utilizing every available surface is a must. Any flat surface can become a drink holder, an eating surface, a bar, or a place for storage. That desk in the living room? Clear off the top, and use it as a snack table. Coffee tables, end tables, and ottomans make for good serving tables, too.

Just try to space out where you set up these distinct areas, so your guests don't end up crowded in one corner. Having different areas encourages movement and flow, and promotes easy access to serving areas and socializing.

Remember that not everyone needs a seat. This is a party, not a work meeting, so don't go out to buy or borrow chairs that will simply clutter the room. Instead, work with what you have. Many guests will stand for most of the evening, so push the sofa and chairs against the walls to create an open space in the center of the room, arranging the seating in small clusters to create intimate corners.

Clear your sofa of space-stealing pillows to make more room for guests, and instead try stacking the pillows on the floor to encourage people to sit there if they choose.

MAKE SPACE FOR COATS AND BAGS

Setting aside a designated spot for guests' belongings is a good idea to avoid unnecessary items lying around taking up valuable party space. Clear out your front hall closet for coats, or buy or borrow a foldable coat rack. You can even place it in the communal hallway so guests can hang up their outer layer before they walk in—but remember to let your neighbors know first.

TAKE IT OUTSIDE

If you're lucky enough to have an outdoor space in your home, be sure to utilize it.

Keep the porch, balcony, or patio open for mingling, weather permitting. Using this space gives your guests the opportunity to get some fresh air, and it really opens up the party so people don't feel confined to one room. Decorate these areas with pretty lights, paper lanterns, and balloons so that guests know they're part of the party too. Even if the weather is a little gloomy, consider keeping a window or two open for airflow so it doesn't get too stuffy inside.

"If we're going to be friends let's get one thing straight right now. I hate snoops!"

MAKE A MINI BAR

Fixing up a small designated area for drinks is better than sending people off to the kitchen every time they need a refill. And as the bar often ends up being the focal point of the party, place yours in a spot that's easy to access. Select a piece of furniture that's wide and roughly waist-high to form a counter. Dressers, side tables, desks, and console tables can all work well.

Place a sign on the bar directing beer drinkers to the fridge, or try a large bucket filled with ice on the floor. Spreading around the booze also minimizes the chance that too many people will be waiting for a drink at the same time. Secure the bottle opener to the front of the fridge with a magnet, or tie it to the bucket handle so people can open their own bottles.

For those who may not be drinkers, have pitchers of ice water handy, and refill them regularly for people to help themselves. Passing around water is also a sensible idea if people are drinking alcohol. Add slices of lemon, lime, or cucumber to liven it up.

WHAT NOT TO SERVE

For a cocktail party, anything hot or too elaborate can cause extra stress. Apartments tend to be on the hot side at parties in any case, so don't turn yours into a sauna by turning on the oven. Instead, stick with room-temperature offerings. Great crowd-pleasers include platters of cold meats, cheeses, olives, fruit, breads, and crackers.

Remember that your snack placement will determine the circulation patterns of your guests! So spread them around the room in different spots to ensure that guests don't end up clustering in one corner to get food. Also be sure to provide snacks that accommodate any of your guests' food allergies.

LIGHTEN UP

For evening parties, keep the lighting low and flattering to encourage a relaxed vibe. If you're having a daytime party, maximize natural light as much as possible to keep your guests awake and energized.

PICK A PLAYLIST

The best music choices tie in with your party occasion or theme, so prepare a playlist beforehand. It's important in a small space to keep the volume quiet enough so people can socialize but loud enough to add atmosphere. Spacing multiple speakers as far apart as possible can help. Later in the party, after everyone has been mingling for a while, turn up the tunes and get the dancing started.

FUN FACT

When filming the famous cocktail party scene, movie director Blake Edwards wanted to capture the freewheeling party lifestyle of Holly and her New York friends as realistically as possible. So he ordered cases of real champagne and let the bubbles flow among the actors, allowing everyone to relax and contribute their own ideas of outrageous behavior. "We really just had a party," he would later say when interviewed about the making of this scene.

Best Ever Breakfast at Tiffany's Cocktail Party

Everyone loves a good house party, and adding a 1960s cocktail theme is a great way to ensure your soiree has both style and class. Cocktail parties don't need to be daunting or mean that you spend the whole evening mixing drinks. The key here is to create one or two signature cocktails that will impress your friends. You can always premake drinks before the party and have them in pitchers, or source vintage punch bowls for that period feel. Here we've got a few cocktail ideas, some authentic food and drink recipes, and a few tricks to make your home really sparkle. Just add your own playlist of early pop classics or retro jazz, including the original Henry Mancini *Breakfast at Tiffany's* movie soundtrack, of course, and you've got everything you need to get guests fully into the '60s swing of it.

Decor

Dig out your holiday fairy lights, and use them to create a magical atmosphere in your chosen party space. Affix around doorways, mantelpieces, and the drinks station for ultimate party lighting. Hang pale blue, white, and black paper lanterns grouped in threes around the room.

The chosen bar area will be key for this party, so dress it with cocktail shakers and a good mixture of thrift-shop glasses. Appropriate retro shapes include martini glasses, champagne coupés and flutes, and cut-glass spirit tumblers.

Handwrite or print out the names and recipes for the three main drinks (pages 136 and 137) on cards, and post them on walls behind the drinks station, so people know what's available.

SPARKLING MARTINI GLASS CENTERPIECE

Make this eye-catching centerpiece to spruce up your next cocktail party's decor.

WHAT YOU'LL NEED

- Oversize plastic martini glass (available online or from party supply stores)
- Silver tray or plate
- Roll of pearl string (medium to large pearls)
- Retro silver cocktail shaker
- Rhinestone tiara
- Pair of oversize sunglasses
- Large bag of large plastic rhinestone gems

Place the martini glass on the silver tray, and fill it with the pearl string so that some strands spill out and hang in loops out of the glass, draping down the sides. Set the cocktail shaker firmly on top of the pearls, and place the tiara and sunglasses on either side. Finally, sprinkle the loose rhinestones all around the bottom of the glass and on the silver tray. Place on the bar or in another strategic spot where guests will see it.

Personal Touch

Knowing the power of a personal touch, Holly handwrote her invitation to Paul for drinks in beautiful lettering. Follow her lead by using an old-style ink pen to handwrite invitations on plain white cards. Channel your inner Golightly and write: "Darling, you're invited to cocktails..." Then include the date, time, location, and RSVP information. Post or deliver by hand.

Drinks

MARVELOUS MISSISSIPPI PUNCH

Inspired by Holly's Southern roots and the
punch she serves at her cocktail soiree, this
whiskey-and-orange-based drink is sure to
get the party started!

YIELD: 14 SERVINGS

- 2 bottles dry white wine (such as chardonnay), chilled
- 1½ cups grenadine, chilled
- 1½ cups bourbon, chilled
- 1 cup fresh orange juice, chilled
- 1 cup cranberry juice, chilled
- Juice of 12 limes
- 8 cups ice cubes
- 1½ cups lemonade, chilled
- 1 cup club soda, chilled
- 2 oranges, sliced thinly

Pour the wine, grenadine, bourbon,
orange juice, cranberry juice, and lime
juice into a pretty punch bowl. Stir in ice
cubes, lemonade, and club soda. Add the
orange slices.

Place the bowl on a small side table with a
large ladle and a supply of colored mugs—
just like Holly does at her soiree—so guests
can help themselves.

"I suppose you think I'm very brazen or très fou or something."

—HOLLY GOLIGHTLY

"I don't think you're any fou-er than anyone else."

—PAUL VARJAK

WHITE ANGEL WITH LYCHEE AND ROSE PETALS

It's said to be Holly's favorite cocktail, and our version of this classic is picture perfect with decorative pink petals.

YIELD: 1 BEVERAGE

- 2 ounces vodka
- 1 ounce gin
- 15 ounces lychee syrup or liqueur
- Crushed ice
- Edible pink rose petals, for garnish

Combine vodka, gin, and lychee syrup or liqueur together with crushed ice in a cocktail shaker. Shake and pour into a classic martini glass, and serve with two or three rose petals floating on top.

BLUE VIRGIN FIZZ

This recipe is a simple way to make anyone not drinking alcohol get the *Tiffany's* treatment.

YIELD: 64 OUNCES

- Blue food coloring
- 64 ounces lemonade, chilled

Add a few drops of food coloring to a large jug of old-fashioned lemonade, and serve chilled in champagne coupé glasses.

Snacks

PIGS IN BLANKETS

These vintage sausage snacks became popular party food in the late '50s and early '60s after a recipe was published in a best-selling cookbook in 1957.

YIELD: 50 PIGS IN BLANKETS

- 2 packs ready-made puff pastry
- 25 mini sausages
- 25 mini vegetarian sausages
- 1 egg, lightly whisked

Preheat the oven to 400°F. Line a baking sheet with parchment paper.

Roll out the puff pastry on a lightly floured surface until it reaches approximately 11 by 14 inches. Cut into 1-inch strips (more or less, depending on the size of your sausages). Cut the strips into thirds, and roll each piece around a sausage. Pinch the seam to seal it. Place it on the baking sheet, seam side down. After all the sausages have been wrapped, brush them with the egg to add a glossy finish, and bake for 15 minutes, until golden brown. Serve warm on a raised plate.

THE ULTIMATE COCKTAIL PLATTER

Keep your guests' stomachs from rumbling with these '60s-inspired party favorites.

YIELD: 1 PLATTER

- 2 to 3 pounds sliced cold cuts of various types
- 1 pound sliced cheeses of various types (for example, one hard, one smoked, one Swiss)
- 1 bunch red seedless grapes
- 1 bunch green seedless grapes
- 1 jar pitted olives

Place the olives in a small bowl in the center of the serving tray. Roll the meat slices into cylinders, and place them vertically to the long side of the platter. Leave about an inch of space between meats. Layer the slices of cheese in the middle of the serving tray, between the meats. Leave an inch of space between the cheeses and the meats. Line grapes between the meat sections. Offer toothpicks for guests to use.

Dress Code: Hollywood Glam

This vintage-style get-together deserves high glamour. Don't be afraid to ask guests to come in cocktail attire. Now's your chance to wear your little black dress and kitten heels, and use all the Holly-inspired tips from the fashion, beauty, and hair chapters of this book. Think beehives, long gloves, pearls, and rhinestones—basically, what Holly would wear! And try the Golightly Evening Glamour makeup tutorial on page 42.

Holly Golightly Champagne Brunch

Breakfast is a special time for Holly. We see her enjoy Danish pastries, coffee, champagne, and, on one occasion, milk shared with Cat and drunk from a champagne glass. Of course, no one feels like throwing a party first thing in the morning, so our *Breakfast at Tiffany's* get-together is a more civilized midmorning meal. This means dressing up Holly-style and gathering your friends for delicious pastries, decadent drinks, and gorgeous pearl decorations—all pulled together with a beautiful shade of blue running throughout. And once you've all had your fill of food, laughter, and bubbles, settle in on the sofa for a screening of *Breakfast at Tiffany's*.

"I don't think I've ever drunk champagne before breakfast before. With breakfast on several occasions, but never before."

—PAUL VARJAK

Decor

Cover the dining table with a white linen cloth, and add a black-and-white striped table runner down the center.

For the centerpiece, arrange a display of eight to ten white roses or four to five heads of white hydrangeas in a small, low vase. Then place the vase inside an open blue gift-style box. Tie a large white ribbon around the base of the box and finish with a neat white bow.

Use a black or pale blue charger plate underneath each white dinner plate.

Set a champagne coupé glass for each guest. Roll pale blue napkins neatly, and tie each with a string of pearls. Rolls of faux pearls can be purchased at many craft shops.

FAUX PEARL PLACE CARDS

Make every guest feel special with these personalized pearl place holders.

WHAT YOU'LL NEED

- One 2-inch Styrofoam ball for each guest
- Can of pearl-white spray paint
- Disposable cups
- Silver pipe cleaners, 1 for each guest
- Hot-glue gun
- 2 sheets black card stock cut into 2-by-3-inch pieces
- Silver pen
- Craft knife

Spray each Styrofoam ball with pearl-white spray paint, and leave to dry, resting in a disposable cup. Fold a silver pipe cleaner into a ring, and hot-glue the "pearl" to the pipe cleaner. On each piece of black card, use a silver pen to write a name card for each guest. Use the craft knife to cut a slit in the top of the pearl ring. Slide the name tag into the slit and place one at each table setting.

TOP TIP

Have a pot of fresh coffee available so guests can enjoy Holly's Danish-and-coffee breakfast combination. For a cute touch, you can even serve it in cardboard takeaway cups!

Drinks

MILK & HONEY BREAKFAST SMOOTHIES

Sip a delicious creamy smoothie from a champagne glass, just like Holly does with her morning milk in the film.

YIELD: 4 SMOOTHIES

- 2 cups plain yogurt
- 2 cups milk
- 1 tablespoon honey
- 1 banana
- Cinnamon, to sprinkle

Place yogurt, milk, honey, and banana in a blender. Blend until smooth and creamy. Pour into coupé glasses. Sprinkle with cinnamon for garnish, and serve.

PALE BLUE MIMOSAS

Holly likes to start the day with champagne on occasion, and so can you with this delicious lemony cocktail—complete with its eye-catching movie-inspired pale blue color.

YIELD: 8 MIMOSAS

- 2 tablespoons white sugar
- ½ lemon
- ¼ cup blue curaçao
- 1 bottle sparkling white wine, such as champagne or prosecco
- 2 cups lemonade

Place the sugar on a small shallow plate. Run the lemon around the top of each champagne flute, then dip and coat each rim in sugar. Mix the blue curaçao, sparkling wine, and lemonade in a pitcher, and stir. Pour into champagne flutes to serve.

Brunch Dishes

NEW YORK–STYLE EGGS ROYALE WITH SMOKED SALMON

A Manhattan classic, these creamy eggs make the perfect brunch treat.

YIELD: 4 SERVINGS

FOR THE HOLLANDAISE SAUCE
- 3 egg yolks
- ¼ teaspoon Dijon mustard
- 2 teaspoons lemon juice
- 2 teaspoons white wine vinegar
- ½ cup butter

FOR THE EGGS
- 4 eggs
- 2 English muffins, sliced in half
- 8 slices smoked salmon, cut in small slivers
- Salt and freshly ground black pepper
- Handful of chopped chives

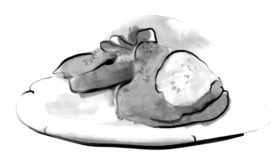

TO MAKE THE SAUCE

Combine egg yolks, mustard, lemon juice, and vinegar in a small blender, and cover. Pulse for a few seconds to combine, and set aside.

Melt butter in a glass bowl in the microwave.

With the blender on high, slowly pour butter into the egg yolk mixture. It will start to thicken immediately. Keep blending until all the butter has been added.

Turn off the blender, and set sauce aside.

TO MAKE THE EGGS

Bring a small pot of water to a boil, then reduce heat until water is just slightly simmering. Poach the eggs in water for 3 minutes each or until whites have cooked through.

Lightly toast the sliced English muffins, and place one half on each of four plates.

Spoon half a tablespoon of sauce onto each muffin half, then top with one poached egg. Add a quarter of the smoked salmon slivers on top of each egg.

Drizzle the remaining sauce over the eggs, dividing equally between the four plates. Top with a little salt and black pepper and a sprinkling of chopped chives onto each.

HOLLY'S CINNAMON & RAISIN DANISH SWIRLS

Make your own easy version of the treat Holly nibbles as she gazes into the shop window in the opening scene of *Breakfast at Tiffany's*.

YIELD: 12 SWIRLS

FOR THE ROLLS
- 1 package refrigerated puff pastry
- 1 tablespoon butter, softened
- ⅓ cup sugar
- 1 tablespoon ground cinnamon
- ¼ cup raisins
- 2 tablespoons milk, for the glaze

FOR THE ICING
- ¾ cup powdered sugar
- 2 tablespoons hot water
- ½ teaspoon vanilla extract
- Piping bag and tip

BONUS!

Brighten up your table with a vibrant fresh-fruit platter—thin slices of pineapple, apples, and kiwi, whole grapes, strawberries, blueberries, and pomegranate seeds. Arrange them beautifully on a plain white dish.

Preheat the oven to 450°F. Line a baking sheet with parchment paper.

TO MAKE THE ROLLS
Unwrap the pastry, and roll it out on a lightly floured surface into a 10-by-8-inch rectangle. Spread the softened butter over the pastry in a thin layer.

Combine the sugar and cinnamon in a small bowl, and sprinkle evenly over the pastry. Sprinkle the raisins on top.

Starting from the shorter edge, carefully roll up the pastry into a log, creating a spiral pattern when viewed crosswise. Cut the log into 1-inch slices.

Lay slices onto the lined baking sheet, spiral facing up, and brush a little milk onto each roll to form a nice shiny glaze as it cooks. Bake for 10 to 12 minutes, until golden. Leave to cool for 30 minutes.

WHILE THE PASTRIES ARE COOLING, MAKE THE ICING
In a small bowl, mix powdered sugar, hot water, and vanilla extract until smooth. Transfer to a piping bag, and pipe long lines across the pastry to finish, leaving to set before eating. Arrange on a tiered cake stand to serve.

Dress Code: '60s Daytime Chic

There are two looks from the film to use for this party inspo. First, Holly's outfit when she goes shopping with Paul consists of a belted fine-knit dress and a statement belted bright orange coat. This vintage Chanel vibe feels very Jackie Kennedy. Alternatively, just because the sun is up, there's no reason you can't take inspiration from Holly's evening style and rock a little black or hot pink party dress. The choice is yours! Head back to the fashion chapters for some ideas on clothes, hair, and makeup to suit this occasion.

For Fun

If possible, borrow or rent a screen and projector to create a classic Hollywood atmosphere when you sit down to watch the film. If you can't procure a screen, a blank white wall will also work. Place your projector appropriately to achieve a picture that is as large as possible but still clear. Keep in mind that the farther a projector is from the viewing screen the bigger the image, but the closer it is to the screen, the clearer the image will be. Place a sofa opposite the screen or wall, or scatter comfy floor cushions on the ground. Have bags of popcorn at the ready.

"This is some party. Who are all these people, anyhow?"

—PAUL VARJAK

"Who knows? The word gets out."

—HOLLY GOLIGHTLY

Gift Bag Ideas

Fill a paper gift bag for each guest to take home with some or all of the following:

· Box of Cracker Jacks
· Mini Cat figure
· String of faux pearls
· Rhinestone earrings
· Oversize black sunglasses from a discount store
· Cat and dog masks like those Paul and Holly steal in the film. Can't find exact replicas online? Some websites offer free templates you can use to print your own— just add elasticized string at the sides.

Pajama & Pearls Pamper Party

Nobody rocks boudoir chic quite like Holly—so who better to inspire a perfect pajama and pampering party for your closest friends? For this night of *Breakfast at Tiffany's* fun, we show you how to set up a 1960s beauty salon in your living space. This is a great party to host in the winter months, when snuggling up in cozy clothes with warm drinks and yummy treats will make you forget the chilly weather. And, of course, no pajama party would be complete without Holly-style eye masks and earplugs, which you'll find along with other indulgent goodies in our party bag suggestions. So follow our easy party plan and make it an at-home spa night to remember.

Decor

If you have one and are able, clear your dressing table and mirror, and bring it into the party space to use for the main table display. Otherwise any table surface will do. For the table centerpiece, source a black jewelry display hand—available inexpensively online. Hang a pale blue silk eye mask from the fingers, along with a long pearl necklace, wrapped a few times, for a nod to our heroine, Holly. Then fill a large old-fashioned glass-lidded jar with cotton balls in pastel shades. Complete the display with two or three beautiful vintage perfume bottles and a selection of retro-looking nail polishes.

BEAUTY STATION

For that special-occasion feel, hire one or two local mobile beauticians for the evening—many offer party rates, and you can share the cost among the group. Or, if a professional isn't in your budget, just take turns pampering one another. Print a treatment card on pale blue paper, and in fancy black or silver ink, list what's available at your home salon.

FOR EXAMPLE:

TONIGHT'S TOP *TIFFANY'S* TREATMENTS

- Marvelous Manicures
- Perfect Pedicures
- Relaxing Shoulder, Foot, and Hand Massages
- Eye-Brightening Treatments
- Silky Hair Conditioners
- Skin-Smoothing Face Masks

TOP TIP

Use some of the DIY beauty product recipes from Chapter 2, whipping them up together during the party, including the mask recipe on the following page.

"Now, that, indeed, is a remarkable piece of information to have at your fingertips."

PEARL PORE-PERFECTING MASK

This treatment contains real ground pearl particles, which are said to brighten and nourish skin and have been used in skin care as far back as Cleopatra's time. Make this mask as a group activity, then sit back and relax while you leave it to work its magic.

YIELD: 1 MASK

- 1 tablespoon pearl powder (available online or in health food stores)
- 1 vitamin E capsule
- 1½ teaspoons rose water

In a small bowl, mix the pearl powder with the oil from the vitamin E capsule, adding rose water to make a paste. Then apply the mixture to a cleansed face, using fingers or a makeup brush, and leave for 15 minutes. Wipe off with a damp washcloth.

Drinks

HOLLY'S TIPSY HOT TODDY

Containing delicious bourbon, this bedtime drink is both warming and soothing.

YIELD: 12 DRINKS

- 9 cups water
- 1 to 2 cups bourbon (depending on how boozy you want it to be!)
- 3 to 4 tablespoons honey, to taste
- Juice of 2 lemons, plus 1 lemon sliced into rounds
- 1 teaspoon ground cloves
- 1 teaspoon ground nutmeg
- 12 cinnamon sticks, for garnish

Bring the water to a simmer in a large pot. Add the bourbon, honey, lemon juice, cloves, and nutmeg, and stir. Sample to check for sweetness. Add more bourbon, honey, or lemon juice to taste.

Serve in glass mugs with a cinnamon stick stirrer and a slice of lemon over the edge.

SLEEPY TIME TEA

The herbs in this tea recipe are all said to have soothing and relaxing properties to ease stress and help get you in the mood for restful sleep.

YIELD: 12 CUPS

- 8 to 9 cups water
- 4 teaspoons dried chamomile flowers
- 2 teaspoons dried mint leaves
- 2 teaspoons dried lemon balm
- 3 teaspoons dried lavender flowers
- Honey, to taste

Bring the water to a simmer in a pot, and add chamomile flowers, mint leaves, lemon balm, and lavender flowers. Turn off the heat, and leave to steep for 5 minutes. Strain through a tea strainer.

Serve in a vintage-style silver teapot and pour into teacups. Place a bowl of honey and a spoon on the side for guests who prefer a sweeter taste.

TOP TIP

Herbs for the Sleepy Time Tea are available online or from health food stores. Or you can buy a ready-mixed bag of loose-leaf tea containing some of these relaxing ingredients.

Snacks

MINI HAMBURGER HEAVENS

Holly meets Sally Tomato's "lawyer" in Hamburger Heaven to pass on the coded weather reports from the jailed gangster, so these delicious snacks are a nod to the film that movie fans will love.

YIELD: 24 HAMBURGERS

- 2½ pounds ground beef
- 1 teaspoon each of salt and cracked black pepper
- Butter, for frying
- 12 cheese slices, cut in half
- 24 mini burger buns or small bread rolls, split
- Ketchup, for topping

Place the beef in a medium-size bowl, add the salt and pepper, and mix. Divide into 24 equal-size portions, and shape each portion into a patty.

Heat a griddle pan on medium-high. Add enough butter to lightly coat the pan, using a spatula to spread it over the base. Add the patties and cook for 3 minutes, until brown, then flip and add a cheese slice. Cook for an additional 2 to 3 minutes, or until cooked to your liking.

Place the burgers in the buns, and serve immediately on a wooden food platter with a dollop of ketchup on each.

MIDNIGHT FEAST CANDY JAR

Buy a large old-fashioned glass candy jar with a screw-top lid, and fill with a mixture of any pale blue, black, and white candies. Candy can be bought in bulk online at good prices. This touch is a knowing nod to the fact that Holly used to call Sally Tomato "my candy store" because she earned an impressive $100 per week visiting him in jail.

LULA MAE'S CHOCOLATE CHIP COOKIES & MILK

Cookies and milk before bed are a comforting treat that can make even the most sophisticated grown-ups feel nostalgic, safe, and loved! This recipe recalls Holly's past life as Lula Mae, stealing milk and eggs to feed her brother Fred.

YIELD: 24 COOKIES

- ½ cup butter, softened
- ⅓ cup granulated sugar
- ½ cup packed brown sugar
- 2 large eggs
- 1 teaspoon vanilla extract
- 1 teaspoon baking soda
- 1 teaspoon salt
- 1½ cups all-purpose flour
- 2 cups semisweet chocolate chips
- Cold milk, for serving

Preheat the oven to 350°F, and line a baking sheet with parchment paper.

Cream the butter, granulated sugar, and brown sugar with a hand mixer or stand mixer fitted with the paddle attachment until well-combined. Add in the eggs and vanilla extract, and beat until light and fluffy. Mix in the baking soda and salt, then slowly stir in the flour and mix until the batter is smooth and comes together. Be sure to scrape the sides of the bowl during mixing. Slowly mix in the chocolate chips.

Spoon balls of dough about 2 tablespoons in size onto the lined baking sheet, spacing them 2 inches apart. Bake for 10 to 13 minutes, or until light golden. Leave to cool for 10 minutes, and serve with cold milk in retro glasses of your choice.

TOP TIP

Make the cookie dough a day ahead, and keep it covered in the fridge until you need it.

Dress Code

Any beautiful nightwear will do, but for authenticity, encourage guests to come in crisp white (or pastel) cotton pajamas—or, for that full Holly look, a men's long dress shirt! Complete the look with silk robes or bathrobes and fluffy old-fashioned slippers.

For Fun

Holly and Paul spent their first real date doing things they'd never done before around New York City, starting with drinking champagne before breakfast. Ask every guest to make a list of three things they've never done before, then share these wishes with the group. Brainstorm how to make these dreams come true. The game isn't finished until everyone has made a promise to complete one of their firsts—or as Holly would say when extracting a firm commitment: "Cross your heart and kiss your elbow!"

"I've never been for a walk in the morning before. At least not since I've been in New York. I've walked up Fifth Avenue at six o'clock, but as far as I'm concerned, that's still night."

"But just look at the goodies she brought with her."

Gift Bags

Hand out these fun treats to your guests as they arrive. If possible, use blue bags tied with a white ribbon. Each bag could contain any or all of the following:

- A silky eye mask, à la Holly
- Tasseled earplugs (see page 27 for how to make your own)
- Sheet face mask
- Mini nail polish in pale blue
- Mini bottle of champagne or prosecco with a paper or reusable straw

Use these pages for your own entertaining notes.

Conclusion

"Is she or isn't she?" When Hollywood agent O.J. Berman bumps into Paul Varjak at Holly's cocktail party, he wants to know if the young writer agrees that their perfectly polished hostess must be some kind of phony. When Paul gallantly takes exception to this description of the spirited young woman for whom he is already falling, Berman demurs: "She is a phony. But on the other hand, you're right. She isn't a phony, because she's a *real* phony. She believes all this crap that she believes. You can't talk her out of it."

As a description for the inimitable Holly Golightly, "real phony" falls some way short. But it is true that beneath the effortless grace and breezy personality, people close to Holly can see the hard work she has put into becoming the ultimate social butterfly. After all, it was O.J. Berman who gave Lula Mae Barnes a year's worth of French lessons to help her lose her thick Texas accent—only for Holly to ditch the idea of becoming an actress altogether!

The Holly we meet may put up a veneer of carefree frivolity, and even world-weary cynicism at times, but as Paul discovers, she is really just a young woman trying to work out her place in the world. She's making it up as she goes along, with as much style and brio as she can muster. In other words, Holly Golightly is more than just an impossibly perfect, unattainable icon—she's also just like us.

Holly tries very hard to pass off her approach to life as entirely spontaneous, but as Berman tells Paul, there is a bit more art to it than that. Like us, Holly is a trier. And there's absolutely nothing wrong with that.

Hopefully you'll try out many of the beauty and fashion ideas within the pages of this book. Perhaps you're inspired to channel some of Holly's signature style, from her hair tricks to hostess tips. With practice and planning, your best efforts may appear as effortless as Holly's.

But, as the movie's closing scene makes clear, ultimately it is perhaps even more important to get in touch with your inner Holly, that mix of grace and gumption that made us fall in love with Miss Golightly in the first place.

Some days the perfect, messy bed head takes two hours of styling to look un-styled. On bad hair days, your only hope is a hat! And on those darker days when the mean reds threaten to surface, it's time to dig deep, and tap into your own inner Holly, your core self-belief, and find some true style and confidence. Because you never know what could be "waiting round the bend." Perhaps your own Hollywood ending lies just across Moon River.

INSIGHT EDITIONS

PO Box 3088

San Rafael, CA 94912

www.insighteditions.com

Find us on Facebook: www.facebook.com/InsightEditions

Follow us on Twitter: @insighteditions

ISBN: 978-1-68383-858-6

Publisher: Raoul Goff

VP of Licensing and Partnerships: Vanessa Lopez

VP of Creative: Chrissy Kwasnik

VP of Manufacturing: Alix Nicholaeff

Designer: Judy Wiatrek Trum

Associate Editor: Anna Wostenberg

Managing Editor: Lauren LePera

Production Editor: Jennifer Bentham

Production Director/Subsidiary Rights: Lina s Palma

Production Manager: Eden Orlesky

ROOTS of PEACE   REPLANTED PAPER

Insight Editions, in association with Roots of Peace, will plant two trees for each tree used in the
manufacturing of this book. Roots of Peace is an internationally renowned humanitarian organization
dedicated to eradicating land mines worldwide and converting war-torn lands into productive farms and
wildlife habitats. Roots of Peace will plant two million fruit and nut trees in Afghanistan and provide farmers
there with the skills and support necessary for sustainable land use.

Manufactured in China by Insight Editions

10 9 8 7 6 5 4 3 2 1